CANADIAN REVIVAL:
IT'S OUR TURN

CANADIAN REVIVAL:
IT'S OUR TURN

George Mallone

WELCH PUBLISHING COMPANY INC.
Burlington, Ontario, Canada

Scripture quotations in *Canadian Revival: It's Our Turn* are taken from the New American Standard Bible unless otherwise indicated.

ISBN 0 920413 10 2

Welch Publishing Company Inc.
960 Gateway
Burlington, Ontario
L7L 5K7 Canada

Printed in Canada

CONTENTS

To The Late David Watson,
Who Aided Many In Overcoming The Barriers To Renewal,
And Gave Hope For Revival In Canada.

FOREWORD

Canada is my country now, so I read George Mallone's book as a word of personal address. I hope that other Canadians will read it in the same way.

Divine revival, God's quickening visitation of his moribund church, is something that we can neither predict or precipitate. But we can and should seek it directly, and be willing to pay the price of so doing, when we see it to be needed. George Mallone understands this well, and spells it out with force.

A few of the norms which he states or implies would be disputed in some quarters, and seem to me, I confess, somewhat doubtful. But to shrug off his book for this reason would be a spiritual cop-out. His thrust is not academic, but prophetic and practical, and the question for us is not whether he makes his point in a safe and guarded way, but whether he has received a vision — that is, true insight — from God: insight to which all Canadian Christians should give heed. I think he has, and therefore wish his book the widest possible readership. It could be a landmark in the spiritual history of our country. May it be so!

James Packer

PREFACE

It was one of the worst winters in Canadian history when Bob Birch and I set out on a tour of seventeen Canadian cities. Thirty days later we had interviewed three hundred pastors and church leaders and spoken to over two thousand people.

One would be crazy to subject his body to flying every thirty-six hours, trying to sleep in a new bed every other night, eating at all odd hours of the day, and pushing twelve to fifteen hours every day, unless there was a great cause at stake. Bob and I had such a belief.

The summer before our trip I had been reading of a similar journey across Canada taken by a young man named J. Edwin Orr. In 1935, Orr traveled coast to coast trying to assess what God was doing spiritually in this country. He recorded his journey in a little book called *Times Of Refreshing: 10,000 Miracle Miles Through Canada*.

After reading the book I was compelled by the Holy Spirit to attempt a similar journey. The night the idea was born in my spirit I called Bob Birch and asked him to consider joining me. Normally one would think twice about asking a seventy-four year old man to join you on such an arduous trip, but I knew him to have twice my energy and a great desire to see revival come to Canada. It was a perfect match of young visionary and old dreamer (Acts 2:17).

Our central purpose was to attempt to hear what the Spirit was saying to the church in Canada. We realized at the outset that we had prejudices and desires for our trip. What we believed to be important in Vancouver might not be viewed as important in another city. To the best of our ability we gave these preferences up to the Lord and asked for insight to see what He was doing, no matter what the label on the bottle said. This conviction led us to many small and unknown Christian works as well as to the offices of large denominations.

The evidence from our trip, as well as testimony from other sources, convinced Bob and me that the country was in desperate need of genuine revival.[1] *It's Our Turn* states that conviction and describes not only some of the things we saw, but a biblical response to them.

Maybe you are new to the Christian faith and not so familiar with what is going on in Canada today. Here is a brief introduction to the subject and an overview of the book.

Most Canadians have had some contact with the church, but over the last twenty years this contact has been less and less frequent. There are two outstanding reasons for this exodus.

First, the growth of man-centered philosophies has precluded the necessity of the Christian view of God, his word the Bible, and the acceptability of people who follow these standards. To be a Christian is not an "in" thing in Canada, although it used to be. It is now academically frowned upon, said to be the source of many of our "hang-ups", and compared to modern morality, it is out of date. Because of this assault many have left the teaching and the practice of the church.

Second, is the decline of the church itself. It is obvious from observation that people are leaving the church because it is perceived as irrelevant to our day and especially hostile to change. The overnight collapse of many mainline denominations and the loss of influence of the Roman Catholic church, suggests that the church needs to preach to itself, to clean up its own act and to be the people God intended. Only then will we win the right to speak to a skeptical generation.

A survey of the book looks something like this. Chapters one to three define revival and the obstacles we face to it in Canada. Chapters four and five address the issue of spiritual warfare, the enemies' opposition to revival. Chapters six through eleven describe specific conditions that are needed for revival: repentance, power in the Holy Spirit, a new form of evangelism, unity in the church, effective intercessory prayer, and political activism. Chapter twelve is your opportunity to respond to God's call for Canadian revival.

My deep appreciation goes out to Burnaby Christian Fellowship and Emmanuel Christian Community for financing our trip across Canada and allowing me time to write our response. My heartfelt love goes out to my delightful wife Bonnie who managed three young children in my absence. She is the human bonfire that keeps my spirit warm. I am indebted to my good friends in Vancouver, especially the pastors in the Wednesday prayer fellowship, who have believed and prayed with me for the revival of the church in Canada. Betty Feeley, Lorraine Schoel and Peter Davids graciously gave their services to nurse my computer, especially during its period of amnesia. Bruce Robertson, Don MacLeod, and at the last minute J. Edwin Orr, took time to read the manuscript and made valuable suggestions. Last, I owe much to my colleague and beloved father in the Lord, Bob Birch, who had to put up with me for thirty days and now has to see me everyday at Burnaby Christian Fellowship.

PENTECOST SUNDAY, 1984

1   P.J. Johnstone, *Operation World: A Handbook For World Intercessors* (Bromley and Kent, England: STL Publications, 1978) p.52.

Chapter 1

WHO CARES FOR CANADA?

A British newspaper ran a contest to determine the most sensational headline that could ever be written. Readers were asked to send captions of not more than four words. The authoress Dorothy Parker submitted her humorous and arresting banner in just two words: "Pope Elopes!"

If such a contest were held in Canada, I believe the most sensational headline would be: "Canadian Church Revived!"

In the last three hundred years there have been demonstrations of God's divine work in this country, but never a progressive coast to coast awakening. Unlike our European parents and American sister, revival has not been part of our religious consciousness.

This is not to say that Canada has not been sympathetic, nor a promoter of revival. In fact, Canada can rightly be called the mother of the Second Evangelical Awakening which swept the eastern United States, Wales, Ireland and Scotland (1858-9). Scholars suggest that one million people were added to the American church in just two years as a result of this revival. And where did that revival begin? Hamilton, Ontario!

Dr. Walter Palmer, a wealthy doctor turned evangelist, and his wife Phoebe became known to Canadian Methodists in the early 1850's for their camp meetings in Ontario. In late September (1857) the Palmers were on their way to Albany, New York and had planned to stay only a night in Hamilton. However, as it occasionally happens today in our modern airline travel, their baggage was misplaced and they were forced to stay longer with friends.

With this inconvenience came an invitation to speak to a united gathering of three Methodist churches. Those who came to the first meeting were challenged to begin praying for revival and some thirty people made this a personal covenant. On Friday night October 2, the first meeting was held and twenty-one conversions were reported. During that week only one sermon was preached by Dr. Palmer and the remainder of the time was given to exhortations from Phoebe and testimonies by laymen. At the end of six weeks, attendance at the three Methodist churches increased by over one thousand, the majority being new conversions to Christ.

After the first two weeks, news of the revival reached New York City and sparked the famous noon hour prayer meetings in which ten thousand businessmen met to pray. Sad to say for Canadians, the revival which began in Canada was mostly reaped in the United States and Europe.

WORST REVIVAL EVER!

A Canadian received a letter from a Christian friend living in the southern part of the United States. The letter had one revealing comment: "We just completed our spring revival and it was the worst revival we have ever had."

Such a comment reflects the shallowness of our understanding of the word revival. Revival is thought to be a style of meeting which if properly conducted will lead to the conversion of sinners. It can be pre-planned, packaged and transported by a few anointed and industrious individuals. But such a man-centered definition falls short of not only the biblical perspective but also the picture given to us from church history.

Revival is first and foremost an activity of God which is initiated, directed, and sustained by him, and intended solely for his glory. Revival from beginning to end is God-centered.

J.I. Packer has defined revival in God-centered terms with the following five-fold definition:

1. Revival is when *God comes down* and is beheld in his infinite holiness, majesty and power (Isa. 6:1-5).

2. Revival is when *God's word comes home* with divine authority to correct our spiritual formation and aid us to behold the face of Christ (Heb. 4:12-13; 2 Cor. 17-18).

16

3. Revival is when *God's purity comes through* by quickening our conscience to see the gravity of our sin as well as the magnitude of God's love and forgiveness (Ps. 32:1-7).

4. Revival is when *God's people come alive.* "Joyful assurance of salvation, conscious communion with the living Saviour, a spirit of prayer and praise, a readiness to share with other believers, and a love that reaches out to all in need, are the characteristic marks of revived Christians" (Acts 2:41-47).

5. Revival is when *outsiders come in* "drawn by the moral and spiritual magnetism of what goes on in the church" (John 13:34; 17:20-21).[1]

Agreeing with Packer's God-centered approach, let me add a few functional dimensions to our concept of Canadian revival.

REVITALIZED SPIRITUAL LIFE

First, Canadian revival will lead to the *revitalizing of the spiritual life* of every superficial and lethargic Christian. There will be an infusion of God's presence by his Spirit which will cause people to make a lengthy inspection of their life, to turn around from willful disobedience and to pursue the goals and character of the Kingdom of God.

This renewal will be a whole person renewal, touching every aspect of life. The inward journeys of repentance, prayer, meditation, Bible reading, and personal worship will be enhanced. The relational journey of parents towards children, spouses towards one another, employers towards employees, and believers to believers will be reconciled and restored. The outward journey of sharing Christ with non-Christian friends will no longer be a dreaded obligation but a delightful joy. Opportunities for social responsibility, both local, national and international will be cherished and promoted.

RESHAPED STRUCTURES

Second, Canadian revival will *reshape the personality and structure of our local congregations.* Jesus' condemnation of the Pharisaical tradition that "the old is good enough" (Luke 5:39) applies likewise to the church. Each man-made tradition of the church will be examined in the light of Scripture and its relevancy to this generation. The

reformation concept that the "reformed church is always reform-
ing" will not be viewed as a threat but as a God-sent blessing.

CHURCH UNITY

Third, Canadian revival will once again set into motion the desire of
believers to fulfill Jesus' prayer for the *unity of his church* (John
17:20-23). The goal will not be the formation of new institutions with
agreement at the lowest common denominator, nor the obliteration
of denominational distinctions and heritage, but a visible display of
loving relationships and fraternal partnership in the common goals
of the Kingdom.

GREAT MISSIONARY FORCE

Fourth, Canadian revival will mean profound repentance by believers, the *conversion of millions of Canadians, the planting of thousands
of new churches, and the sending of a great missionary army* into the
rest of the unreached world.

Canadian revival should not be interpreted as a movement
towards emotionalism. Surely emotions will be stirred and sometimes erratic in such a renewal, but this is not its essence. Neither will
revival mean a return to primitivism, the notion that the church can
replicate exactly the situation of the first century church. This is the
twentieth century and any renewal which takes place in it must be
free of past provincialisms. Canadian revival will not mean the
pushing of revivalistic techniques, the whipping up of dedication on
some yearly basis only to be forgotten the next. No, if revival comes
to Canada it will be something God has set in motion and nothing
for which man can take glory or assume pride.

SIX STEPS TO CARING

Taking a "man in the street" survey, a reporter asked a rushing
pedestrian: "Sir, do you know the two greatest problems in the
world today?" "I don't know and I don't care!" responded the
hurried man. Without losing a beat the reporter replied, "You got
them both!"

Although God is sovereign in his dispensing of revival, it still
needs to be asked of every Canadian, "Do we care for this country?

Do we care that God would work in our midst? Do we care that God would be glorified in this nation?"

Nehemiah was a man who cared about his own country and was overwhelmed by its need for revival. For a number of years he lived a quiet and comfortable life in Susa as the cup bearer to the Persian king Artaxerxes (Neh. 1:1,11; 2:1). But when his brother Hanani brought news of the poor conditions of the Jews in Jerusalem (1:2-3), Nehemiah began to pray and plan for Jerusalem's restoration.

Today, few of us are Nehemiahs. For us to have this concern for Canada would take an exceptional work of grace. But we should not underestimate the possibility that God could work his grace upon us. An admirer of Theodore Roosevelt once exclaimed, "Mr. Roosevelt, you're a great man." Roosevelt responded honestly and said, "No, Teddy Roosevelt is a simple, plain, ordinary man; but highly motivated."[2] Although the number of concerned Canadians is growing, there is still room for thousands of people to be highly motivated for the concern of Canadian revival.

At this point a problem arises. How do we learn to value what God values, when we are not naturally motivated to value it? If we are not Nehemiahs now, how do we become so? The following six principles can apply to numerous areas of life; in this section they are exclusively focused on the application to Canadian revival. How is it possible for me to value the revival of God's people in Canada when I am not presently motivated to this end?

First, *acknowledge your lack of care for Canada's spiritual health* and confess your failure to assume your God-given responsibility. Jeremiah 12:10-11 tells us why the country lies in desolation.

> Many shepherds have ruined my vineyard. They have trampled down my field; They have made my pleasant field a desolate wilderness. It has been made a desolation. Desolate, it mourns before me: the whole land has been made desolate, because no man lays it to heart.

When we came to Christ, each of us took on a mantle of leadership in God's royal priesthood (1 Peter 2:9), leadership for ourselves and leadership for other people (e.g., family, neighbours, Christian community). If the country lies in ruins it is because we have not taken our God-ordained leadership seriously. Instead of the "buck stops here" we have adopted the attitude of "have buck, will pass."

19

We have not taken Canada's plight to heart. Everyone assumes that it is someone else's responsibility and not their's to own. But 2 Chronicles 7:14 lays the burden of the nation on all the people of God, not just a select few. "If my people who are called by my name humble themselves and pray, and seek my face and turn from their wicked ways, then I will hear from heaven, will forgive their sin and will heal their land."

God already knows our inadequacy in this area. He knows that we have not cared, that we have not prayed and that we have not yet turned from our wicked ways. He only wants us to acknowledge our failure. The New Testatment word for confession means to agree with God, to say the same thing (1 John 1:9). This is not a simple verbal process that takes little time or reflection, but it must be an acknowledgement which has come from a careful consideration of our motivation and priorities. Our personal sin has crowded out God's concern for the work of the Kingdom in this nation. Confess that sin before him now. Name the idols which have held you in check. Acknowledge your responsibility for the spiritual desolation which is Canada.

Second, *acknowledge that your choice is the major ingredient the Holy Spirit will use* to motivate you to be concerned for Canada. The Holy Spirit does not co-opt choice, he cooperates with choice. He will not move if you do not move. Scripture assumes that believers have within their reach the ability to obey what God commands of them, so acknowledge that your choices are important to Canadian revival.

Third, affirm by faith that *God's word has the solution for the desolate Canadian church.* Holy Scripture is our guide for renewal (Ps. 119:25). There may be hundreds of ideas for overcoming the inadequacy of the Canadian church: reports from committees, trained specialists for problem areas, and comments from the suggestion box in the vestibule, all with varying degrees of helpfulness. But only God's Word is the unalterable truth for the church's dilemma. Scripture has much to say about the church, what it is to be and what it is to do. The question we must pose for ourselves is, are we conforming to the God-given directions and affirming God's Word as our solution?

Fourth, by faith, *picture in your mind what it would be like to obey God's Word* in our concern for Canada. Envision what it would be like to begin the daily practice of confession and repentance for known sin. Picture what it would be like for you to love the members of Christ's body as he loves the church. Imagine what it would be like if all the Christians in your city were really one as the Father and Son are one. Contemplate the notion of one thousand new converts coming to your church next week and millions throughout the country turning to Christ. Some of the pictures are no doubt overwhelming and full of logistical headaches, but they are also full of great personal blessing.

Fifth, *affirm God's Word by doing what it says.* You do it because it's truthful and right, not because you feel like it. You do it because God says so, not because you are attracted to do it. You do it because there is no other way the Canadian church can be revived. The remaining sections of this book describe some of the things we can do, so we must roll up our sleeves and do them.

Last, when you consistently do what God's Word says, you will find that your feelings change and that you *actually begin to value what God values.* Proper experience flows when right behaviour is performed. As we take these steps for Canada (e.g., prayer, unity, love, proclamation and service) we shall find our hearts slowly being changed to be like Nehemiah; broken, humbled, prayerful, thoughtfully planning and working the strategy which God provides.

The bottom line for Canada is quite clear. We have never had coast to coast revival in this nation and we need it now. Revival is God's sovereign work which affects believers and unbelievers alike. God's gracious disposition is always towards revival and he only looks to see if there is a people who care enough to pay the cost. At this very moment in history, the winds of revival are beginning to blow in this country. Now is the time to sanctify ourselves, for tomorrow God will do wonders among us (Joshua 3:5).

Who cares for Canada? Don't you?

1   J.I. Packer, "Renewal or Revival," *RENEWAL*, (April-May, 1976) 62, pp.14-17.
2   As quoted in Charles R. Swindoll, *Hand Me Another Brick* (New York: Bantam Books, 1981) p.3.

Chapter 2

REVIVE US AGAIN!

A psychologist sat down with his patient to give his diagnosis. "I have some good news for you and some bad news," he said. "The good news is that you have a strong healthy ego. The bad news is that it doesn't have any basis in reality."

I don't want to sound like an overly critical psychologist, but the same statement could be made of the Canadian church today. Most Canadian Christians have not given any thought to this subject and assume that the church is doing just fine, growing like her American sister and sending numerous missionaries overseas.

In certain places in Canada this is so. From my own observation on a trip across Canada as well as from reading and speaking with others, it would appear that the Canadian church is progressing in at least six areas: in several of the Western provinces; among native Indians; among handicapped and prisoners; in ethnic churches of some of our larger cities; and among the French speaking population of Quebec. However, in other parts of the country the church appears to be standing still or declining.

Before we look more closely at the need for Canadian revival, let us consider the meaning of the Psalmist's words, "Wilt Thou not Thyself revive us again, that Thy people may rejoice in Thee?" (Ps. 85:6).

PRAYER FOR RESURRECTION

When the Greek version of the Old Testament translates the word "revive" it uses a word which means "to turn" or "to turn back." However, the Hebrew word used here is much more striking, suggesting the resurrection of the dead. In 1 Kings 17:22, Elijah prays over the widow's deceased son and scripture says that "the Lord heard the voice of Elijah, and the life of the child returned to him and he revived." In 2 Kings 13:21 a dead man is thrown into the grave of Elisha and the moment the dead man touched the bones of Elisha "he revived and stood up on his feet."

What is needed in Canada today is a resurrection, not just a slight turning, or a mere alteration of our machinery and outlook.

Theologically, resurrection is no problem for God. God's present problem is to get Canadian Christians to lay down and admit that they are dead. Jesus' word to the church at Sardis is so appropriate for us today: "I know your deeds, that you have a name that you are alive, and you are dead" (Rev. 3:1).

HOW NEEDY IS THE CANADIAN CHURCH?

Living on the border of the United States creates a false religious security among Canadians. We think that since we are so close and "children of a common mother" we have the same religious fever as do the Americans. At this moment, I have on my desk an article from *Time* which says that there are fifty-nine million evangelical Protestants in the United States.[1] That is one out of every four Americans claiming to be a Bible believing, born-again, church practising Christian.

How many evangelicals do you think there are in Canada today, a country of some twenty-five million people? Approximately 20% of our population are practising Roman Catholic (some 5 million), 3.4% attend (not belong to) mainline churches (e.g., Anglican, United Church of Canada, Presbyterian — approximately one million), and 3.5% attend conservative evangelical churches (e.g., Baptist, Pentecostal and others — approximately one million). From an evangelical perspective the number of born-again Christians in mainline denominations is only guess-work, and likewise for the number of genuine Christians in the Roman Catholic church, but participating evangelical Protestants at the most would probably number no more than one and one-half million.[2]

But it is the bottom line which is most disturbing. Eighteen million Canadians, over 70% of the population, are unchurched non-

Christians. Canada is not like the United States because we under-evangelized country.

However, this is only part of the disturbing news. If we gated a little more we would probably find that some 80% to 90% of these eighteen million Canadians have had some contact with the Christian church, Protestant or Catholic, and have rejected its influence. Through baptism, Sunday school classes, clubs or marriage, their contact has only been superficial and nostalgic. And so we can rightly conclude that Canada is overrun by baptized and secularist non-Christians or unchurched non-Christians.

Canadian universities have approximately 680,000 students. Inter-Varsity Christian Fellowship, which is one of the oldest and most respected student witnesses in Canada, ministers to some three thousand students. If we take the other para-church works on campus: Campus Crusade for Christ, Navigators, and various other student groups, we would probably have no more than ten thousand students active in Christian groups on campuses. Certainly one must consider that most Canadian students live at home and commute. Given this assumption and the fact that most Christian students spend more time with their home church than they do on campus, even when we are generous it still means that 500,000 students do not know Christ.

In one of our major cities there are forty junior and secondary high schools. Out of the forty schools only five have active Christian witnesses. The overwhelming majority of our public schools are unreached by the gospel. There are exceptions: the various religious schools in Newfoundland, and Quebec and the exceptional efforts of a small band of committed Christian teachers who lead clubs on their campuses, and the few schools which have the services of groups like Young Life and Youth for Christ, but all of these are rare when given the overall picture.

CHURCH GROWTH OR DECLINE?

"Organized religion in Canada is experiencing a dramatic drop-off" says Lethbridge sociologist Reginald Bibby. "Churches are losing many of their once-active members and adherents, while failing to replenish such losses."[3] In making this assessment Bibby surveyed 2,000 people across the nation from mainline and Catholic churches.

At the very same time evangelical churches in Canada seemed to be experiencing increased numbers. In many cities large new sanctuaries are being built by evangelicals which can seat one to three thousand people. Many of these churches claim that they are "growing". The numbers are there to be sure, but where have they come from?

It is my suspicion that many of these churches are growing from three sources. First, people are leaving mainline churches because of the absence of evangelical doctrine and practise (thus some of the 3.4% are joining with the 3.5%). Second, growth is occurring from smaller evangelical churches which cannot offer the services, plant or program available through a larger church (thus a fluctuation of the denominational numbers in the 3.5%). Third, there are increased numbers from churches leaving the downtown cores of their cities and building in the suburbs.

Is the church growing in Canada? With the exceptions given in the first part of this chapter, I think we must say no. New churches are not being planted to reach unreached people. The sheep are only migrating from pasture to pasture. The tide of secularism is beating against the walls of the church and some are already falling.

CAN THESE CANADIAN BONES LIVE?

Ezekiel was an exile in Babylon, when he was called to be God's prophet. As a divine spokesman he had seen God in his awesome majesty and he had also seen the wickedness and depravity of rebellious Israel. For six years he preached the inevitable judgment for their sins. Israel had now fallen into captivity, but in that position God brought a new message to Ezekiel. "The hand of the Lord was upon me, and He brought me out by the Spirit and set me down in the middle of the valleys; and it was full of bones. And he caused me to pass among them round about, and behold there were very many on the surface of the valley; and lo, they were very dry" (37:1-2).

We should note first of all that it is the Spirit which enabled Ezekiel to see the dry bones. Let it be known that this is of itself a work of grace, for the enemy does not want us to see the dry bones. He wants to flatter us and fool us about the reality of the Canadian church. He wants us to ride on the glory coattails of our American sister, to read only the articles which pertain to successful Canadian churches and to pass out copies of Dean Kelly's *Why Conservative Churches Are Growing* to all our "liberal" friends. He wants us to do anything but to look at these dry Canadian bones.[4]

If this is not a sufficient deterrent to our investigation, then our own carnal man rises up to defend nominality. He whispers in our ears, "Canadians are not fanatics. Remember your British tradition. Form a Royal Commission!" Or "Let's keep religion in its place. Out of sight and out of mind." But the Holy Spirit wants us to see the dry Canadian bones, for then and only then will we be able to cry out like Israel, "Our bones are dried up, and our hope has perished. We are completely cut off" (37:11).

Catherine Marshall gives us a hint why this confession is so necessary when she says, "God is a realist and insists that we be realists too. So long as we are deluding ourselves that human resources can supply our hearts desires, we are believing a lie. And it is impossible for prayers to be answered out of a foundation of self-deception and untruth."[5]

Ezekiel noticed two other things about these bones. First, they are not linked together in a body as they were created to be and second, they lie bleached white and dry.

Probably the single greatest discovery of the doctrine of the church in this century will be the confession that the church is a community, a family, and not just an institution. Surely we must have some organization and program, but the essence of the church is relationships. The body of Christ, each different part, living in a harmonious and upbuilding manner with one another (Eph. 4:11-16).

Many of us were raised listening to the "Lone Ranger" on radio, but did you ever think that the Lone Ranger was never really alone?[6] He had Tonto to rescue him countless times. But Tonto, which means "dimwit", was never really seen by the Lone Ranger as an integral part of the process. So many Christians have lived this same way in the body of Christ: alone, independent, self-sufficient and scorning any Tonto that would help. But God did not call us to himself to be disconnected dry bones. He called us to be part of his body, his new family nurturing one another.

O LORD, THOU KNOWEST

God spoke to Ezekiel and asked him, "Son of Man, can these bones live (37:3)?" Hesitantly, and probably implying the negative, Ezekiel responds, "O Lord, Thou knowest."

27

Can these Canadian bones live? I believe that God wants them to live. I believe that Jesus wants to come back to a beautiful Canadian bride. I believe that God wants more Canadian children brought into the family. But for this to be a reality we must prophesy over the dry bones, "O dry bones, hear the word of the Lord" (37:4).

It makes precious little difference whether you believe that all preaching is prophecy or that prophecy is very different from preaching. What is incumbent upon each of us is a spoken word which is contoured in humility, free from provincialism, fearless in the face of conventionalism and powerful enough to overcome nominality. Only that kind of word will bring life to these Canadian bones.

Ezekiel was faithful to speak God's word of rejoining the bones (37:7-3), but one cannot miss the humor in the statement that there was much noise and rattling when the bones began to rejoin. "I will go to church with the brother, but I won't love him or relate to him (rattle, rattle)." "We had a good church here, pastor, until you started preaching all this love for one another. Now all you've done is make us mad (rattle, rattle)." "I love my church and my denomination, but I don't like those Christians across the street. They make me nervous (rattle, rattle)."

When God issues a call for the body to come together, he means that it should happen at every level. Congregations should function as a family together. They should then relate to other churches, both within and without their denominational structure. They should also relate to the whole church in their city, for when God views the church he does not think of Anglican, Baptist or Catholic, he sees the church in the city (e.g., St. John's, Winnipeg, Vancouver). In addition each church should have a living relationship with other churches in Canada. As Christians and Canadians we need to know what God is doing in our land. Last, there should be some international link with the church throughout the world so that we realize that we are part of a world-wide family. To bring all these bones together will produce much rattling, but this is what happens when dead bones are resurrected and life is given.

ARTIFICIAL OR GENUINE?

My former secretary had in her dining room a large cabinet filled with china she has collected from around the world. One day a five year old visitor stopped in front of the cabinet and exclaimed, "Mrs.

Spruston, you's got the nicest tupperware I've ever seen!" That little friend had seen the artificial for so long that he did not know the genuine when he saw it.

The same can be said of the Canadian church. For so long we have called dry, disconnected and dispirited bones a church. But this is not the church. The church is a family which is connected together in loving relationships. The church is where the Spirit rules with power, reconciling and restoring, reconstructing broken lives. We can thank God for all we have in Canada today, but that should not deter us from beseeching more of God's blessing for ourselves and those who do not know him.

1   "Counting Every Soul on Earth," *Time* (May 3, 1982) p. 90-92.
2   David Hartzfeld, "Household of Faith," *His Dominion* (Fall, 1981) p. 21.
3   R. Bibby, "The Incredible State of Canada's Largest Protestant Denomination," *Christianity Today* (Feb. 19, 1982) p. 28-30.
4   Dean Kelly, *Why Conservative Churches Are Growing*, (New York: Harper and Row, 1972).
5   Catherine Marshall, *Adventures in Prayer*, (Old Tappan, New Jersey: Spire Books, 1976) p. 19-20.
6   Justo L. Gonzales and Catherine G. Gonzales, *Liberation Preaching* (Nashville: Abingdon, 1980) p. 50.

Chapter 3

IT AIN'T LIKE IT USED TO BE

"O Lord, Thou didst show favour to Thy land; Thou
didst restore the captivity of Jacob. Thou didst forgive the
iniquity of Thy people; Thou didst cover all their sin. Thou
didst withdraw all Thy furies; Thou didst turn away from
Thy burning anger." (Ps. 85:1-3)

In chapter two we concentrated on the phrase "revive us again"
from Psalm 85:6. In this chapter we want to step back and look at the
context for these words and discover one of the many hindrances to
revival.

Psalm 85 was penned by one of the sons of Korah, the clan tribe of
Levites who were responsible for guarding the temple as well as
music ministry within the temple. Likely this Psalm was sung, verses
1-7 by the congregation and verses 8-13 as a solo by one of the
priests.

NOSTALGIA OF THE PAST

The verbs in these three verses are best rendered as a simple past
tense: "Lord, you did all these things for us." Most likely this is a
post-exilic Psalm. Israel had returned from the Babylonian captivity
and was at first delighted by their deliverance. But now it appears
that they are somewhat bitter because the experience has turned out
different from what they imagined. There is a sense that God worked
in the past, but the plaguing question remains: "Where is he now?"

31

These verses are intended to be a recollection of past mercies, leading to prayer. However, one suspects that Israel began to recite these verses as a recollection of past glories, leading them to dream of seeing past situations recreated. In Psalm 44:1,9 we hear another word from the sons of Korah which sounds very similar: "O God, we have heard with our ears, our fathers have told us, the work thou didst in their days, in the days of old ... yet thou hast rejected us and brought us in to dishonour, and dost not go out with our armies."

Instead of recalling the past mercies of God, they are overwhelmed by the nostalgia of the past and are saying to one another, "It ain't like it used to be!" No doubt these returnees sat down and shared with one another the way God had worked so gloriously in the past. He had worked miraculously on Cyrus and on Artaxerxes to allow their return (Ezra 1:1; Neh. 2:1). As they prayed and fasted at the river Aahava (Ezra 8:21) God undertook to protect them from ambush and allowed them safely to smuggle into Jerusalem over one thousand pounds of gold and silver. A great movement of repentance was launched when Ezra humbled himself before God and began to weep over the nation. From that moment people began to clean up their lives and put away things that had been forbidden by the Old Testament law (Ezra 10:1). The Spirit of God had fallen on Haggai and Zechariah and used them for the rebuilding of the temple and at this point God graciously sent Nehemiah to be governor in Israel. In spite of great opposition, the protective walls surrounding Jerusalem were built, the word of God was taught with much authority and people began to order their lives according to God's dictates.

These were the good old days. The days when God was moving dramatically among His people. It was sweet to recall those good old days because they were the only comfort that people had in days which were lethargic and uneventful.

No doubt you, like myself, long for a mighty work of God in our own time, but do you know that one of the major obstacles to this transpiring is nostalgia? Nostalgia of the past only leads to storytelling and dreaming and does not motivate us to pray.

CANADIAN NOSTALGIA

As I toured Canada I was amazed with the number of times in conversation that Canadian nostalgia was used to avoid the reality of the present. It was as though you could justify the present by claiming that the past was better. Let me give you a few examples of both explicit and subtle Canadian nostalgia.

In Alberta, some can be caught saying, "I'll never forget what Aberhart said!" In one place where I repeated this line in public, it was greeted by applause. From some in the Christian Missionary and Alliance you hear, "A.W. Tozer once said....", and from the Fellowship Baptists it is the words of T.T. Shields. Every denomination seems to have one great spokesperson of the past who inhabits the hallways of all their churches. A picture of William Booth seemed to be ever present in all the Salvation Army buildings we visited. But I wonder if we would have thought that a particular quote, or concept or even the person was as important as we make them out to be now, if we had heard and seen them when they originally spoke the word and lived. History has a way of sanctifying words and making the author of those words bigger than real life.

Every pastor knows the nostalgia of the former pastor. "When Reverend Brown was here we used to...." Reverend Brown may have only pastored the church for four or five years or may have been dead over a decade, but his name is evoked as a placard of better times.

In Saskatoon we learned of a different kind of nostalgia, the wistfulness of a bygone revival. When we asked certain pastors what was presently happening in their city they responded, "Nothing has happened here since the revival of 1971." With glorious examples they could describe the benefits of the one hundred and eighty day visitation given to that city, but now little or nothing seemed to be happening (we learned later from our own investigation that several creative and fresh works of the Holy Spirit were going on in the city). As I began to probe the lasting results of the revival, and there were many, I was made aware that you just don't criticize a past revival. You can praise it, but you cannot critique it. The same could be said of the past impact of the Ontario Keswick and the Toronto Spiritual Life Conference.

Many parachurch works have staff members that have been around since the inception of the movement. Rightly so, each year their stock value rises in the eyes of their supporters. Soon they are living legends in their own time. Christians remember fondly their growth experience when Miss White led their group or Mr. Johnson took them to summer camp.

PAST: HINDRANCE OR HELP?

What is the point of these brief examples? It is certainly not that we should sit down and attempt to criticize everything of our past. To focus on criticizing the past will mean that we lose the present as well as the future. We are to respect our history, our tradition, and those who laboured before us. Our ministry today is the fruit of those who laboured before us. But at the same time we are not to live in the past nor let the past govern the present nor the future. History has much to teach us, but it also has much to hinder us. If our urgency is to recreate history or to follow fervently our tradition, then we lose the cutting edge of what God wants to do by His Spirit today. I know these things personally.

In 1971, at the height of the Jesus movement, my wife and I gathered with twenty-five university students to do discipleship training among new converts. In four months, fifteen thousand high school students had professed faith in Christ through the efforts of several churches in our city. We felt it our obligation to launch a ministry of Bible study and prayer for the maturing of these students. In ten weeks our ministry grew one hundred fold. That summer was "manna panic," there were so many people coming to Christ and wanting nurture that we could not manage to meet all the needs. However, in September of that year my wife and I moved to Canada where things were much more subdued and quiet. In our first year, we longed for the dynamic movement which had been with us in the previous months. To our detriment, we ate, slept and drank the nostalgia of the past. But God will not let any of us live in the past for long. To have a living touch with God demands we hear "today" what the Spirit is saying to the Church (Heb. 3:7, 15; 4:7). Any generation which turns to God and pleads his mercy, rather than dreaming or sharing glory stories of the past, that generation can be revived.

DIVISION: THE GREAT CANADIAN FOLLY

One afternoon I was busy studying in my office when I received a phone call from my wife. "There's a terrible storm! The trees are blowing over, and it's hailing, and the children are terrified!" Humorously I thanked her for her concern for me, dry and warm where I was at the time, that she would now want me to venture into the cold rain and come home early. Looking out my third story office window westward towards home I could see the storm alright, with dark grey clouds covering the coastline. Yet from my vantage point I could see something which she was unable to see. Behind the cloudy line the sun had begun to break through. On the phone I assured her in prophetic tones that the worst would soon be over because the sunshine was coming.

In Psalm 85:8, one of the priests performed a similar ministry. Israel needed a prophetic word, someone to stand outside the circumstances and to give a clear perspective on the problem. In the origination of this psalm, no doubt the priest went off by himself to "hear what the Lord will say." What would be God's response to the petition that he would revive his people in order that they might rejoice in him?

After a period of reflection, the priest returned and sang his message to the congregation (85:8-13). The essence of his message was peace, "peace to the godly ones." In modern Hebrew, shalom means hello or goodby. Of the 250 usages of shalom in the Old Testament approximately 60 refer to the absence of warfare. However, shalom has a more relational aspect than this. It means a state of personal and corporate fulfillment, of wholeness when God is present. While doing some study on this word I was arrested by one particular line defining shalom: "unimpaired relationships with others and fulfillment in one's undertaking."[1]

Why is shalom, "unimpaired relationships with others and fulfillment in one's undertaking" such a special word to the church in Canada? Because the absence of shalom has been the historical folly of the Canadian church and is another major hindrance to revival.

MOSAIC OR MELTING POT?

This country has prided itself on being a cultural mosaic rather than a melting pot. But mosaics do have some unsightly aspects, namely the cracks which separate the parts from one another. Canada is divided linguistically, culturally, geographically, and religiously and the church in Canada has been divided since it was first planted in this country.

Take for example the planting of the church in the Maritime provinces. Any excuse at all was reason for Christians to divide. The style of the service or the form of church government caused division. Whether you believed in revival techniques or subdued religion caused schism. Did you favour an itinerant preacher or a local parish priest? Did you advocate union with the government or separation of church and state? Did you cater to the upper class professional people or to common working folk? Did you believe in trained clergy or in the exclusive use of unschooled laymen? Did you believe the gifts of the Holy Spirit had ceased with the Apostles or were they still given to the church? Anything that could be discussed and divided over was promptly done.[2]

Newlight Baptist split from Congregationalist, Salvationist split from Methodist. Methodist split from Anglican. Pentecostals split from Methodist. Brethren split from the Baptist. The result is that today Canadian Christians are the disturbed children of religiously divorced parents. The 3.5% in conservative churches do not relate to one another but remain in their ethnic, denominational and theological ghettos. They also refuse contact with the 3.4% mainline church people and the 20% Roman Catholics!

My concern is not to launch a super-denomination which takes everyone into its fold, but for all believers in Christ in each Canadian city and across the country to live in unimpaired relationships with one another and in the fulfillment of the gospel mandate.

IMPAIRED RELATIONSHIPS

Presently, in Canada there are examples of Christians cooperating with one another for the advancement of the Kingdom, some of these we will mention later. But for the moment let me describe for you some of the pain I observed from impaired Canadian relationships.

In Calgary a group of charismatic Anglican priests told us of the frustration they had with their pentecostal brothers. Whenever they met for prayer, the Anglicans always felt the pressure to be more exuberant and expressive. The subtle pressure was always there suggesting that they should come out of the Anglican church and commune with the genuine believing church.

As twenty pastors sat together in the city of Edmonton, they were shocked as one brother began to cry and confess his loneliness in the ministry. "I've been here for ten years and no one has reached out his hand to me," he shared. The meeting went on to inquire why it is that God's people live in such independence of one another. Billy Graham may pull us together for a crusade, but no sooner than the bills are paid, Christians float back into their isolated domains.

In Saskatoon, it was the frank admission that churches in the city had not worked together since the revival of 1971. In fact, since the revival the churches have grown more competitive with one another, each trying to "outgrow" the other.

"Insular Ontario" was a word we heard often. A province which has such a large percentage of the Canadian population can easily slip into the rut of not needing any input from Christians outside their own province. This attitude filters down to the pastoral and congregational level. At the time of our visit to Toronto, pastors and churches, outside of denomination context, seldom met together for united meetings, prayer or fellowship. One delightful exception was the prayer fellowship that exists among the pastors in Barrie.

I was most anxious to get to the nation's capital, Ottawa. However, from the moment we arrived at the airport we knew intuitively by the Spirit that the city was wrecked with division. This was proven over the next forty-eight hours as we met with charismatics, Catholics, evangelicals and mainline church leaders. Each claimed that the others had no interest in them and would not venture any cooperation. Suspicion, competition and the lack of biblical care for one another was the characteristic of this city. Thankfully, there are a few brave souls who were resisting this tactic of the enemy.

"Proselytism" was a word we heard often in Charlottetown. Many pastors introduced themselves by saying, "I want you to know that I don't believe in sheep stealing!" This was usually followed by an explanation on why such and such a person had moved from church X to church Y. Several times I took the hands of these pastors and said to them: "Brothers, you're not talking to one another. If you would meet together for prayer and worship you might be able to resolve this tension. Your city is hurting because you are divided."

This same competitive spirit was also evident in St. John's, Newfoundland. Primarily it is the Pentecostals versus the Salvation Army. Over and over again people spoke of the conflict these two groups have had with one another over the years.

REVIVED UNITY

Prior to the outpouring of the Holy Spirit on the Moravians in August of 1727, the community at Herrnhut was wrecked with quarreling facts, so much so that the community lay on the brink of disruption. But when the Holy Spirit came, following a communion service, so did the unity of the body of Christ.

Canada is filled with division. Here is an analysis of Canada by Dr. George Peters, former professor of Missions at Dallas Theological Seminary. "As I look at the church in Canada, I see a large group of people who profess to be Christians, but who are not really aware of the presence of God nor of Christ in their lives. They lack spiritual reality. In consequence they do not really know whether they are Christians or not. On the other hand, I see small evangelical groups or a movement struggling, battling its way up and onward. These groups and churches have my deepest sympathy in the visions and goals. However, they are too segmented and scattered into many little groups to be real effective witnesses in their communities."[3]

Can you imagine a war being fought in which the army, navy, and airforce did not talk to one another? Such is an accurate picture of the state of the church in Canada. Division is the great Canadian folly, and along with the nostalgia of the past is the second major hindrance to the revival of the church.

1   Lloyd Carr, "Shalom," *Theological Wordbook of the Old Testament*, (Chicago: Moody Press, 1980) Vol. II., p. 931.
2   S.D. Clark, *Church and Sect In Canada*, (Toronto: University of Toronto Press, 1948).
3   "Interview with George Peters," *His Dominion*, (Spring, 1978) p. 6.

Chapter 4

WE'VE NEVER DONE IT THIS WAY BEFORE

Two men spent the afternoon fishing for trout. One noticed that his friend was saving all the small fish and throwing the large ones back into the stream. Very soon, curiosity got the best of him and he asked about this strange procedure. "I've only got an eight inch frypan for cooking" was his friend's reply. Sounds very much like the thinking of the church, doesn't it? God may be granting great blessing, but our frypan (our institutional program) is not big enough. Is it also possible that our small and limited programs are themselves a hindrance to revival?

In Luke 5:33-39, Jesus states two principles which are absolutely necessary for the church if revival is to come. First, the church is to be responsive to Christ's living headship and not bound by institutional models. Second, the church needs to develop new wineskins in order to contain the new wine of the Gospel. However, we should not be deceived, such action is not as simple as it sounds because renewal often generates controversy.

RESPONDING TO CHRIST, NOT INSTITUTIONS

The Old Testament prescribed fasting only one day of the year, that being the day of atonement (Lev. 16:29,31; 23:27-32). During the exile, four additional fasting days were kept, signifying the national mourning of Israel and the remembrance of the disasters which had overcome them. Pious Jews fasted two days a week (Luke 18:12), Monday and Thursday during the time of Jesus. From the report we have here it would appear that the disciples of John the Baptist were following the same pattern. But the disciples of Jesus did not fast prior to Pentecost; therefore, the accusation that they were always eating and drinking was correct.

Jesus uses this background to allude to a custom whereby attendants at a marriage feast were released from their religious duties during the seven days of festivities. Jesus emphasizes that you cannot compel people to fast during this time, but later they would be released to fast (Luke 5:33-35).

What is Jesus saying to the church with this allusion to the marriage feast? I believe he is suggesting that Christian response is to the living, risen, communicating head of the church and not to a man-made institution. We fast because we long for the presence of Jesus, not because we are institutionally compelled to do so. We are not to be governed by compulsory obligation to our particular tradition, but responsive to the service of our Lord.

One day two men came to the prophet Zechariah (7:1-7) and sought him to enquire of the Lord whether or not they had to maintain the fast days added during the exile. "Must we maintain these institutions that we have practiced so long?" was their question. "I never gave them to you in the first place!" was God's response.

It is a good question for all of us to ask: How many of our practices today are of self-origination? Must we meet at 11:00 a.m. for Christian worship and promptly conclude at 12:00? Must we have a Sunday school program and mid-week prayer meeting? Is a choir an essential part of the church? With many of these programs we can say that God never gave them to us in the first place, but they are just practices that we have always maintained.

Institutions of the church are meant to serve the church and at any point where they begin to bind and dominate the church, they are to be resisted. Flogging people to attend dead and useless programs is no way to disciple people, for it is only the presence of Jesus that can motivate them. Therefore, we must ask, are people having access to the presence of Jesus through this program or is it just a tradition which has now obscured his presence? In responding to Jesus, many of our traditional programs need to cease and in their place we must seek the creative ministries which speak the presence of Jesus to people's needs today.

GOOD ENOUGH?

Why is it that we are so reluctant to change church structures? Jesus suggested that it was our natural tendency to respond that "the old is good enough." The wineskins Jesus had in mind were sewn goatskins which at first were elastic, but with time they deteriorated and became inflexible. The potency of this new wine was guaranteed to give you a double back-flip. What Jesus said was well known in the wine growing communities of Israel: you don't put this powerful fermenting wine into old wineskins, otherwise it will split the skin and the contents will be lost. New wine must be put in new wineskins.

However, it is the last words of the parable that are most revealing, "the old is good enough." There is a textual variation in this phrase. Some Greek texts use the word "better" while others use the word "good enough." The last is the preferred reading. In practice there is a world of difference between these two words. "Good enough" suggests that we have not tried anything new and we are content with what we have. We don't want to venture anything new, so the old is sufficient. But when we say the old is "better" we are saying that we have at least tried something else, but still prefer the old.

Several years ago I officiated at a Chinese wedding. At the banquet meal there were two dozen dishes of exotic Chinese food placed before us. I like Chinese food, but most of this I had never seen before. Out of fear I ate only the things I knew would agree with me, the "old was good enough." However, other guests around the table noticed my reluctance and began to chide me into eating a few of the delicacies. After a few helpings, I pronounced with great authority, "the old is better." So often the church is characterized by the first of these attitudes. Without comparing other programs or new methods, we pronounce the old as sufficient and warrants our singing of the hymnal parody:

> Like a mighty tortoise Moves the church of God
> Brothers we are treading Where we've always trod.

YOU DON'T CHANGE FOR CHANGE'S SAKE

One of the major reasons believers say "the old is good enough" is because of our fear of change. Many churches are afraid of growth, both in numbers and quality of life. Growth means change and there are doubts if we can live with the expectations of the change. We know, through past experience, that we can meet the expectations of the old patterns, but the new potentials leave us quite insecure. Many in local leadership sense they do not have the forethought to design a new alternative nor the ability to lead the congregation in concensus change. Nor do they have the skills of sustaining change. We may be able to lead a Wednesday evening prayer meeting where the pastor does all the talking, but not a meeting in a home where others are allowed to participate.

And all along there is the plaguing question, "What if the change doesn't work?" For many of us this is a direct attack on our humility. We have taught people that we are functioning in the New Testament way and change would mean that we would have to admit that we have been too narrow or even wrong in our practice. Such admission is no easy matter. We do not want to appear foolish or fickle in the eyes of the people.

Change also exposes us to verbal flak from those who are not prepared to move. Usually one of three invalid statements is made in opposition, "You don't change for change's sake!", usually said condescendingly. "You must always march to the beat of the slowest member!", which is said like quoting the church constitution. And last, you can fill in the blank because every region of the country and ethnic group in Canada feels this way, "We____ are slow to change." When these attitudes dominate a church, the leadership usually becomes a thermometer rather than a thermostat, reflecting the heat rather than producing the heat. But spiritual leadership demands that we call people back to Christ as the Lord of our programs. He alone has the right to set our agendas and to lead us into creative avenues of ministry. Any Canadian church that wants to be used for revival must be a church which is flexible to structural change.

RENEWAL EQUALS CONTROVERSY

At no point can we forget that the renewal of the church in spirit and structure is controversial, has always been controversial, and will always be controversial. There is no way to get around it. If we want the church to break forth in new expressions of spiritual life and creative ministry, we must be ready for controversy.

Note these few examples. Nova Scotia was settled by New Englanders with Congregational and Anglican ties. In the later part of the 1700's, God raised up a non-ordained and uneducated preacher to plant dozens of churches in that province. Henry Alline and the New Light movement, however, were constantly criticized by the religious establishment for their fanaticism, divisive preaching, sectarian phrases and violent gestures. Yet, much of Nova Scotia was evangelized through this man and the movement.

In two years (1858-1859), 100,000 people were added to the church in Wales as part of the Second Evangelical Awakening. One of the characteristics of this revival was the use of moliannu, a form of worship which included choruses of rapturous praise. Local police officials took to attending these meetings because people no longer frequented the pubs. And yet the press and many clergy of that day criticized the movement for its emotional hysteria and its undermining of a sense of responsibility, primarily because businesses closed down to attend church meetings.

Pentecostalism, which is today called the "third force in Christianity," began in controversy. Charles Parham preached the "baptism of the Holy Spirit" at the Bethel Bible School in Topeka, Kansas in 1901. Agnes Ozman was the first to receive "the baptism" and later spoke in tongues. Parham and his wife carried the same message throughout the United States for the next three years, but received only opposition and criticism.

From my own limited experience, I have also tasted controversy of renewal. From January to March of 1971, I was immobilized by depression. Deep in my spirit there was a longing for the working of God. Shortly after this time, as I have already shared, approximately 15,000 high school students came to know Jesus Christ. Yet in the midst of our discipleship of these students several families in my own local church became upset and set in motion a heresy trial. My hair was too long, my politics were too liberal and my theology too radical. Revival was breaking out, but so was controversy.

SATAN RAGES

Why is renewal so controversial? Jonathan Edwards is helpful at this point and gives some answers that will prove useful for Canadians as we prepare for revival.[1]

First, *Satan rages* whenever he begins to lose his grip on men and women, and he immediately launches a counter-attack. His strategies are numerous and fierce.[2] He will spawn accusations against leaders of the church. This will either produce an overreaction which places leaders above criticism or an environment in which the leadership is destroyed by unwitting gossip. The devil will attack people through discouragement and depression. He will plant lies and stereotypes in the minds of unbelievers. One of his major caricatures today is that all Christian television personalities are really sideshow hucksters concerned only for money. Failing this maneuver, he will set renewal leaders against one another in order to divide and conquer. He will overbalance the zeal of young converts so they act without knowledge or forethought, running to extremes. And last, he will sow counterfeit revival to distract attention from the genuine work of God.

Second, during revival, many *people are poorly informed* as to what is happening. Unsubstantiated stories begin to move along gossip channels. Soon someone is misquoted, an action is misinterpreted or an activity is misunderstood. Heresay evidence carries along reports which bear no resemblance to the original. No doubt this was the method in which second century pagans concluded that Christians participated in sexual orgies during their "love feasts" (Jude 12). All such accusations come because people are not rightly informed.

Third, many people are offended because they have *not personally experienced renewal*. They are defensive when placed next to those who have. They do a little dance to rationalize and defend their nominal experience. At one moment they are attracted by what they see of renewal, only to react in the next. They realize that there is a cost to renewal and as they dialogue about that sacrifice they find themselves more anxious and confused. "I don't know what it is about you," one man said to me. "I don't like what you are saying, because I'm afraid you're right. If you are right, then my life has to change."

Fourth, renewal *confirms principles people chose not to embrace*. Renewal challenges people not only to think biblically but to act biblically. The literalness of discipleship demands that we embrace practices which we previously spiritualized or ignored. Thus, those who are moved by the Holy Spirit to this exacting discipleship will naturally expose the shallowness of the commitment of others. People will have to admit that the action is biblical and that they are living at a substandard level.

Last, *people become jealous* because they have not been used as instruments in the renewal. Each of us values our usefulness in the Kingdom of God and depending upon the strength of our egocentricity, we value ourselves as important to this work. Yet when someone else appears more productive in ministry, we are immediately beset by jealousy. "Why have we not been used by God?" becomes our cry. "Why, God, have you used them?"

Structural change in the church is controversial. It is much easier to stay with our tried and true programs rather than venture out into any new uncharted waters. It is too easy to offend people by doing something new, so we don't. Spiritual renewal is also controversial. It calls people to reexamine the purity of their lives and the freshness of God's presence with them. Conflict is produced when some begin to make new ventures in their walk with God, so we quietly try to keep a lid on things, hoping that no disruption will take place. Such attitudes keep us from revival. Such attitudes play into the enemy's hand and keep the church in Canada in a comatose state.

1   Jonathan Edwards, "The Distinguishing Marks of a Work of the Spirit of God," *The Works of Jonathan Edwards*, (Edinburgh: Banner of Truth, 1974) vol. 2, pp.259-277.)
2   R.F. Lovelace, *Dynamics Of Spiritual Life*, (Downers Grove: Inter-Varsity Press, 1979) p.41.

Chapter 5

I THINK I CAN

I wonder if you ever read *The Little Engine That Could* by Watty Piper? If you haven't had this pleasant experience, let me tell you the story. It's the story of a little steam engine which comes to the rescue of a big shiny but broken down train. The little engine is called to aid in the urgent mission of carrying toys to the children over the mountain. Although the load is heavy and the hills are very steep, the little engine conquers every challenge by repeating to himself, "I think I can, I think I can."

In the writings of Nehemiah, Israel is much like the little engine carrying a heavy load. But instead of optimistic determination there is negative skepticism, for the people have begun to repeat to themselves:

> "The strength of the burden bearers is failing, Yet there is much rubbish; And we ourselves are unable to rebuild the wall." (Neh. 4:10)

In other words, Israel was repeating "I don't think we can, I don't think we can." Why was this pessimism in Israel? Nehemiah had learned from his brother that the Jews who had returned to Jerusalem after the Babylonian captivity were in distress (Neh. 1:1-3). The walls of Jerusalem were broken down so that they were defenseless in the face of attack from hostile neighbors. Nehemiah secures permission from Artaxerxes to go to Israel and to lead in the rebuilding of the wall (2:1-8). However, before and during the building of the wall, Israel's enemies incited so much opposition that doubts began to arise about the value of the task and the strength to fulfill it.

For the Christian, Nehemiah is not just a story of the building of the literal wall in Jerusalem, it also serves as encouragement to rebuilding the broken walls of our personal lives, our churches and our nation. Any attempt to rebuild, however, will be met by opposition. So Canadian revival will not come unless we are prepared to wrestle that opposition. Nehemiah is helpful to us at this point by revealing three concerns: we have an enemy, but we have authority over that enemy, and we must know the enemy's strategies.

WE HAVE AN ENEMY

When Nehemiah arrived in Jerusalem he discovered that he had stirred a hornet's nest. He was surrounded by opposition — Sanballat and his Samaritans in the north, Tobiah and the Ammonites in the east, Geshem the Arab in the south and the Ashdotites in the west, completely surrounded by those who were displeased that someone would care for the welfare of Israel.

We should not be surprised that the same thing is true in the Canadian church today; only our enemies are not flesh and blood, but strongholds of demonic powers. The Bible says that Christians have an enemy, his name is Satan. He is a fallen angel, who in pride wanted to be God and has declared war on God and his children. He is mighty, violent, intelligent and known for his lying. Although he is powerful, he is not omnipotent. Neither is he everywhere at once or all knowing. He is not incarnate in a person, although many have sold their souls to him and "have become living embodiments of his beastliness."[1] He can enter unbelievers and influence people's minds. He is aligned with the world system of thinking, the promoter of fleshly living and the instigator of demonic activities. He has persuaded 70% of Canadians to read their horoscopes daily and promoted hundreds of witches covens throughout the country.

Satan does not want us to be concerned for the spiritual health of Canada. I found this out when I returned from my trip. The following month I fought depression, resisting the notion that the state of the church was helpless and that Satan had won the day. The writing of this book, two months after the trip has also been a great struggle.

Yes, we have an enemy and he does not want the Canadian church to be revived.

WE HAVE AUTHORITY

When Nehemiah entered Jerusalem, he had two things going for him. First, the king had sent troops along to protect him and second, he had letters of endorsement from the king himself (2:9). The wall was to be rebuilt because the king had given permission and protection. Although the enemies bluffed and threatened Nehemiah constantly, no harm came to him. In the end, the enemies lost confidence and retreated from their assault (6:16).

One of the high school traditions that I treasure in my memory is the tearing down of the goal post after the football game. For most of the year, metal posts were used at both ends of the field, but with the semi-finals and final games, these were replaced by wooded beams. Team victory in one of these games meant an on-rush of people to the field, swaying the posts until they fell and then splintering the post so that everyone had a portion. Everyone needed to walk off the field with a piece of the victory.

The cross of Jesus Christ is the goal post for the Christian. John the Apostle states it this way: "The Son of God appeared for this purpose that he might destroy the works of the devil" (1 John 3:8). He also records these words of Jesus: "now the ruler of this world shall be cast out. And I, if I be lifted up from the earth, will draw all men to myself" (John 12:31-32). Jesus also said that no one could enter the house of a strong man and steal his possessions, unless they had at first tied up the strong man (Mark 3:27).

At the cross Satan overstepped his boundary. He plotted and brought to fruition the death of an innocent and sinless man. He is now condemned by God as a murderer and waiting his day of execution. Because Satan is defeated, though not at this point destroyed, believers have authority over the enemy and can expect that the walls will be rebuilt. As Michael Green suggests, Satan is like a large fish which has been caught, taken aboard ship and had its throat slashed. Frantically kicking about, he refuses to lie down and die. The hostility you and I face in the rebuilding of the wall is the last gasp of a defeated enemy. Violently he strikes out, but he is defeated and the work of God will go forth.

One morning, during the writing of this book and doing some conference ministry, my wife awoke at 3:00 a.m. and sensed a fierce spiritual battle shaping up for the day. Oblivious to her concerns I slept, while she laid my head in her lap and prayed continually for me. When I awoke at 6:00 a.m. the world was spinning in my head. I said to myself that I had a slight vertigo problem and would be over it with a few more moments of sleep. Such was not the case. I forced myself out of bed, showered and had some breakfast. I shouldn't have done the latter, because later I was violently ill, vomiting without any control. As I knelt before the "great white throne", I slammed my hand on the toilet, declaring that I was not about to let the devil defeat that day of ministry. But too ill to move, I could only lie in bed.

About that time a friend called and said that God had told her of my battle and also of my need for a valet to assist me in putting on my spiritual armor. My wife called a pastor friend who came immediately to pray for me. Quietly Bob came into my room and began to take the believer's authority over the evil one. In the name of Jesus, he claimed the binding authority over the devil. As he affirmed this by singing "He is Lord, He is Lord, He is risen from the dead and He is Lord," my body shook with tears. I thought for a moment that I was crying blood because my tears were so unnaturally large my eyes were burning from their flooding. Bob resisted the devil on my behalf and demanded that he flee (James 4:7). My friend reminded me that Jesus alone gives permission for the enemy to engage us (Luke 22:31-32), yet at the same time he prays for us that we will be able to endure. As Bob predicted, I quietly went off to sleep and two hours later I was up, drinking two bottles of pop and driving to a conference where God graciously made Himself known to people on that weekend. The enemy was real, but so was the authority exercised by this believer on my behalf.

STRATEGIES OF THE ENEMY

Billy Martin, who has managed numerous baseball teams in his lifetime, gave this formula for success to *Sports Illustrated*. "You'll have fifteen guys who run through a wall for you, five who hate you and five undecided. The trick is keeping the five who hate you away from the five who are undecided."[2] Like Billy Martin, Christians need to know their enemy's strategy and as well their plan for combatting the assault.

As soon as Nehemiah arrived in Jerusalem, he was met with a wave of verbal mockery from his opponents (2:19). He was even accused of rebellion against the king, even though he had written permission from the king in his possession. In Chapter four we find Sanballat and the others, no doubt at a party, making fun of the poor Israelites. "Those dumb Jews. They don't know how to build a wall. If a fox were to jump on it, the whole thing would collapse" (4:1-3). The strategy of Nehemiah's enemies was to demoralize the builders by sowing words and attitudes which mock and despise.

Another angle of the enemy is to plant a few loafers in the crowd so that everyone else is looking over their shoulder, wondering why others are not working, and longing to be free of the responsibility themselves. Nehemiah had his share of loafers in the rebuilding of the wall (3:5). Likewise, any church which is dominated by comfortable pew sitters or "spiritual welfare bums," is headed for failure. The enemy wants Canadians to remain quiet and inactive, but still in their churches, in order that those who are working hard might be distracted from their work. The enemy encourages church loafers to be near the wall, but not to help rebuild the wall.

In the beginning of this chapter we spoke of the pessimism that was being repeated in Israel, "I don't think we can." Let's look more closely at this little slogan that was being repeated (4:10). "The strength of the burden bearers is failing, yet there is much rubbish; and we ourselves are unable to rebuild the wall." The strength of those working on the wall was failing, yet there was so much more to do. And the more that they discussed what was needed, the more discouraged they became. Certainly one can see this attitude in many Canadian churchmen today. "No progress. No growth. No breakthrough." One friend reflecting this idea suggested that this book should be entitled *The Dumpy Canadian Church*. But we must assign this pessimistic sense of inadequacy to the devil's strategy for discouraging Canadians.

In the midst of rebuilding the wall some of the wives came to Nehemiah with a concern (5:1-13). "Nehemiah, we have some news for you. You can't eat walls. And on top of that, this project of yours is just costing us too much!" Nehemiah continued to listen to find out the source of this rather strong reaction. "You see, it's like this.

Since we have been working on the wall, we have not been pushing the time clock, therefore we have no money to pay the king's income tax. Then one of the good brothers, honest Ben (he has a sign over his door which says: 'Service is our business'), has opened up a pawn shop and he's taking our property and kids in exchange for money to pay the king's tax." Well, Nehemiah was smoked (5:6-7) and he went straightway to confront these brothers. He demanded restitution for those abused and the ceasing of usury, which was already prohibited by Old Testament law (Ex. 22:25).

What's the application for us? It seems that whenever God wants to get his people moving, to spend time building the Kingdom of God, there is always some enterprising Christian who wants to distract us from our primary calling into a venture which is designed to make a little extra money. Sell this or develop that and you will have what you need to be a happy Christian family. But all these "part-time" ventures take time, time which could be used to bring friends to Christ, develop mature disciples, to intercede for the needs for the world and many more nobler causes than making a few extra bucks. Kingdom work takes time and the use of our time is to be one of our priorities.

There was a second internal problem and that revolved around Tobiah, who was a Jew but also a servant of the King of Ammon (2:10) and one of the party goers who had made jokes about Israel (4:3). This man had business contacts with Jews and had relatives through marriage in Jerusalem (6:17-19). While Nehemiah was away, he pulled a few family strings and had gotten for himself a room in the area of the temple (13:6-9). Slowly, but surely, he had begun to infiltrate the Jews and to turn them against Nehemiah. "Gee whiz Nehemiah, Tobiah is a good guy. You should lay off of him. Besides, he's my brother-in-law."

In 4:6-7 we learn that the real intensity of opposition sprung up when the wall was half-way completed. This is intended to cause discouragement in what we've done so far and how far we have yet to go. Any work for Canadian revival can expect opposition and that attack may come not only at the first, but in the middle of such an effort.

Sometimes our enemies come right out and invite us to cease our work. This distraction may be an invitation to leave the work and go meet with the opposition. Nehemiah was invited to the plain of Ono for a discussion, but he knew that Sanballat and the crew meant him harm (6:1-3). Nehemiah's response is still valid today for the invitation of our enemy: "I am doing a great work and I cannot come down. Why should the work stop while I leave it and come down to you?" When revival breaks out, there are plenty of reviewers and critics who want to take time to "analyze" the revival. In those moments, it may be the wisest thing for us to leave them alone and to continue the building for which we were called.

Last, Nehemiah was tempted to sin for a good cause, his own life (6:10-14). Not being a priest he was forbidden entrance to the temple, but Shemaiah had suggested such a procedure since he reported that Nehemiah's enemies were about to kill him. In revival, the enemy will want to persuade us to do wrong in the name of the right, to assume that our ends justify any means. But as Nehemiah knew, such an argument was simply the ploy of the enemy to catch us acting contrary to our own standards. Revival is no excuse for sin.

THE BATTLE IS ON

A few days ago, a stranger called me at the office. Where he got our number I am not sure. After speaking with one of the secretaries for a few minutes he was relayed over to me. He questioned if I knew of a rock concert on television that evening. He went on to state his own position clearly, asking me to pick up the challenge. "Tonight, we're going to worship Satan with this music. You Christians have tried to stop us, but you're not powerful enough. Hundreds of us are now praying and fasting for confusion at the time of your Billy Graham Crusade. We're going to win. You can't defeat us." The fellow's voice was as normal and healthy as you would hear anywhere in Canada. The challenge was very clear. The enemy has already made himself known as our opponent. His strategies are not new and his authority has been broken. We are in a battle and the extent of the Canadian revival will be the extent to which we successfully recognize our enemy and do battle with his host.

1 Michael Green, *I Believe In Satan's Downfall*, (Grand Rapids, Eerdmans, 1981) p.30.
2 as quoted by Ben Patterson, "A Small Pump at the Edge of the Swamp," (*Leadership*, Spring 1980, Volume 1, number 2) p.41.

Chapter 6

WHOLLY FOR GOD

"Sanctify yourselves, for tomorrow I will do wonders among you" (Joshua 3:5).

This one verse has been central in my meditations over the last two years, particularly as I have yearned for Canadian revival. It simply exhorts us to put ourselves in a suitable condition to see the manifest glory and power of God.

There are two elements contained in the verse. First, we must sanctify ourselves. To sanctify something in the Old Testament meant to take an ordinary, common object and set it apart to holy use. Common vessels, like a pot or dish or fork were not holy in themselves, but were viewed as holy by virtue of their separated nature. They were set aside for holy use.

You and I as believers are not holy in and of ourselves, but God calls us saints, *hagios* holy ones (e.g., Rom. 1:7; 1 Cor. 1:2; Eph. 5:3). We are common vessels, set apart for a holy use (2 Cor. 4:7). Although we possess the Spirit of Christ (Rom. 8:9), it is still possible for believers to be carnal (1 Cor. 3:1), to direct their lives to profane use rather than wholly for God. Although we are not told in this verse from Joshua what we must specifically do to sanctify ourselves, we are to take actions which redirect our lives to a holy use for God rather than a profane use for the world.

Second, God promises Joshua that he will do wonders among them. The Hebrew word for wonders refers to things that are unusual, beyond human capabilities, and when they happen they awaken astonishment, fear and awe in people. The same Hebrew word is used in the announcement of Isaac's miraculous birth (Gen. 18:14). The angel announced to Abraham that next year he would have a son. Naturally, at ninety years of age, Sarah felt such an announcement was a bad joke and hence her unbelieving laughter. But the angel responds, "Is anything too hard (too wonderful) for the Lord?" Is there anything beyond human capabilities that God cannot do?

Clearly the wonder in mind for Joshua was the miraculous crossing of the Jordan, even as Moses had led Israel through the Red Sea. Although Joshua did not apparently know this in advance, he was promised by God that sanctifying the people would bear wondrous results.

At this moment in Canadian church history, I believe the same challenge and promise is being offered to us. If we put ourselves in a suitable condition, wholly for God's use, we will see the glory and power of God. I can honestly say today that I have seen more wonders in the last eight weeks than I have seen in the first twenty years of my Christian life. I have seen more people repenting of unholy living, more people making restitution for stolen property and wrong relationships and more people feeling God's healing touch in their bodies than at any other time in my experience. The flow of God's Holy Spirit is clearly moving people to sanctified and wondrous living.

SANCTIFY: AFTER A GREAT DEFEAT

The Old Testament call to sanctification of people is often made after a great defeat (Joshua 7:13), or before a great victory. The prophet Joel gives this exhortation in the context of a past defeat and future victory. He lays out for us a specific plan for revival, a plan that each Canadian church should attempt as soon as possible.

Sanctifying ourselves is something we must do after a great defeat. What was the defeat that brought people back to God in Joel's day? In one word, it was locusts (1:4-7; 2:1-11).

Devastation had engulfed the land. There was drought everywhere, uncontrollable fires and enough locusts to make an Alfred Hitchcock movie. In 1915 a similar plague hit Syria, Israel and the borders of Egypt. *The National Geographic* recorded that event in this way. In March of that year swarms of adult locusts appeared in such "thick clouds as to obscure the sun for the time being." The females began to desposit their eggs in the hard soil, leaving nearly one hundred eggs "neatly arranged in a cylindrical mass" in each four inch hole. "It is estimated by competent authorities that as many as 65,000 to 75,000 locust eggs are concentrated in a square meter of soil." A few days after hatching, the locusts, resembling large black ants began their march "of from 400 to 600 feet per day, clearing the ground of any vegetation before them." *The National Geographic* writers conclude with these words: "Thus Joel, writing some seven or eight hundred years B.C., begins his description of a locust plague, which then as now must have laid waste this land. We marvel how this ancient writer could have given so graphic and true a description of the devastation caused by locusts in so condensed a form."[1]

The locust destruction touched everyone in Israel. The wine-o's had no more drink (1:5). There was no cereal or drink offerings available for the priest to use in the worship liturgy (1:9). The herds were dying and the people were starving (1:17-18).

Twice we are told that the invading army was from the Lord (2:11, 25). Israel had been disobedient to the covenant with God, thus he unleashed the destructive hordes (cf. Deut 28:23, 38; Amos 4:7-9). What disobedience had occurred we do not know, only the effective consequences.

Does God allow this kind of devastation to the church, to those in the New Covenant? Yes, I think so. If we persist in unrepentant sin, giving the devil a foothold in our lives, then God may open his protective hand and let the enemy through, until such time as we repent.

What are the locusts that are eating up this land? I have already mentioned several things in chapters two through four, and I will mention some of the social locusts in chapter eleven. But what are the spiritual locusts that are causing us devastation? I believe five concerns are everywhere evident.

First, there are the forces of *occultism*. Recently in one of our major dailies was a story of a witch with a Ph.D in religious studies. Openly she paraded her crafts under the guise of intellectual respectability and deep mystical powers. This woman met weekly with about thirty other witches to learn their dark secrets and from what we learn from other sources, to pray for the destruction of Christian leaders and the influence of the church. The war is now open for all to see. The prophets of Baal have cloaked themselves in respectability and are now challenging the power of the living God.

Second are *heretical theologians*. Many Canadian seminaries are staffed by men and women who do not walk with Jesus Christ, nor espouse his radical demands for personal discipleship. They have an agenda of their own orgination which expounds more political theory than revealed truth. They are master planners in the deceiving and mocking of truth and have by their leadership devised the bankruptcy of their own denominations. Unwittingly, the average parishioner is financing his own spiritual death through support of these propaganda machines.

Third are *carnal pastors*. Men and women who tolerate sin in their own lives and permit it among the congregation. In order not to cause controversy and the loss of one's job, sin is handled by politics rather than confrontation. One scratches the back of the other and both feel relief, but the disease goes on. When was the last time you saw your own pastor so overcome by his own sin, so repentant of his own failures that he could not go on with things as usual? It is so infrequent because we are so carnal in our professionalism.

Fourth is *misguided women*. There are many Canadian women who do not have spiritual leadership at home and thus have gotten themselves into a position of believing they have heard a word from God and will not submit to anyone. It is a feminist spirit of rebellion that knows submission to no one, especially male leadership in the church. It resists the spiritual intuition of men as being less than adequate to hear the genuine voice of God.

Last are *cowardly men*. For much of my childhood I was a coward, afraid of being hurt and feeling I was too weak, with no skills to fight. One day I was backed into a corner by a huge high school football player. My friends were standing by to see what I would do, and to no doubt pick up the pieces. The shame of being a coward compelled me to give it all I had, and although there was no apparent winner, the chorus of my friends was, "We didn't know you had it in you!" Neither did I. Many Canadian men need to be shamed for their cowardly response to spiritual leadership, both in the home and in the church. The church cries out for brave men, not just lethargic bumps to sit on a committee, but bold men to challenge the devil's domain and take possession of the land by dispossessing the enemy.

When locusts are devouring the land to such an extent that the spiritual and religious life of God's people has nearly ceased, what do we do? How do we sanctify ourselves? Joel provides for us these five steps.

WAIL AND LAMENT

Nine times in Joel's prophecy we are instructed to wail and lament before the Lord (1:8, 9, 13, 14; 2:12, 17). John Wimber of the Vineyard ministries in Anaheim tells a story about a prophecy which launched his church into a ministry of praying for the sick. A woman asked if she could share a word with John, a word she believed from the Lord. As they sat down she began to weep, and kept weeping for thirty minutes. Finally, in some frustration John asked her to cease her display of emotion and get on with the word she had for him. "This is it," she said. "God wants you to know that these tears are how he feels about you!" This dramatic prophecy began in John's life and in many others a ministry of tears for personal sin and for the sick state of the church.

The ministry of tears is not given because of self-pity, or because of a sense of hurt or personal discouragement, but because we have seen the broken heart of the Father for his church and his world. Together with the Father we are crushed to tears by what we see.

There are times in the church in which sin is so ingrained, where hearts are so hard, the only way the Holy Spirit can break up the fallow ground is by the wailing lament of leaders. Bold tears by the church's leadership, tears from a broken and contrite heart can loosen the devil's grip on a carnal Christian.

Canadians across the religious board are not instructed in the ministry of tears. Those who do it often, look like water taps without hearts — turn it on and turn it off. Others not instructed in this ministry run in fear of such an outward display. Good and righteous people don't cry, and if they do, they get hold of themselves very quickly. But if people are repenting of sin, with a choice of their mind and perhaps a display of emotion, let us not interrupt the work of God in order to make ourselves more comfortable. And when our leaders cry out before the Lord, let us not be embarrassed as though some strange event has befallen us. No, it is commendable of leaders to do exactly this when devastation has come upon God's house.

CONSECRATE A FAST

Two times Joel instructs Israel to consecrate a fast (1:14; 2:15). They are to declare a special time for abstaining from solid foods (not liquids) in order to demonstrate the seriousness of their plight before

God. It is a voluntary crisis, a spiritual trauma, in order to realign one's self with the priorities of God. It is a time to intensify the hearing of God's word, and to discipline the control of one's body. Overweight people as well as slender can face the struggle with gluttony, and complusive eating habits. Such a showdown reveals clearly if we are controlling our bodies, or if they are controlling us. Two of the four sins of Sodom (Ezekiel 16:49) related to gluttony and immorality, sins which can only be put to death (Rom. 8:13) by starving them out. "A stuffed belly produces fornication, while a mortified body produces purity."[2]

It is appropriate for every church in Canada to declare a period of fasting for the revival of their own church as well as the church in this nation. It is not an overwhelming project that takes a lot of committees or a large budget. In fact, nothing is needed except people who will forego certain meals in order to show their humility before God and to petition him for revival. Surely this is not too much to ask of any Christian?

SOLEMN ASSEMBLY

In addition to weeping and fasting, Joel calls for the convening of a solemn assembly. This Hebrew word simply means a "stoppage", a halting of our normal work to devote time to spiritual use. It is an extra special time set apart to God, much like a week of Sundays. The solemn assembly may carry on through the night (the fasting of sleep, 1:3) as people are led in repentance and prayer.

Presently, our own fellowship is this month going through such a procedure, with an all-night prayer service at the end of the month and a closing service on the following Sunday. Church activities are purposefully at a minimum so that people can meet together for prayer during this month. We are asking God to reveal areas of sin in our lives that need repentance and also the revelation of the vision he has for us as a church. Again, such a practice would be good for every Christian community in Canada. We need days and weeks set aside to redress our disobedience and to know the marching orders of our Chief Shepherd.

RETURN TO GOD

The purpose of these first three activities (weeping, fasting, and solemn assembly) is not merely religious or liturgical, but to aid us in the process of returning to God. These are physical expressions to assist us in renouncing and disowning lingering sin (2:12-14). Tearing our garments in demonstration of sorrow avails nothing unless there is sorrow in our heart for sinning against God.

The very first word scripture records of John the Baptist is "Repent, for the Kingdom of heaven is at hand" (Matt. 3:2). Mark records that Jesus' early words also contained the same theme: "Repent and believe the gospel" (Mark 1:5).

No doubt this ought also to be one of the first words for Canadian revival. But what does it mean to repent? Repentance for those of different religious traditions can have various meanings. The Greek word for repentance is *metanoeo*. It is a compound word which has the elements of "after" as a prefix and a word which means "mind" or "thought" as the suffix. It means to "change one's mind." On the basis of subsequent knowledge we change and adopt a different view.

Sad to say there is no single English word which catches all the elements of this Greek word, no word to describe the changing of our mind which leads to the changing of our behaviour. Repentance has an unfortunate English connotation of emotional regret or being sorry, but sorrow is not repentance. Often one of my children has come to me after repeatedly transgressing one of the family rules and pleading, "But Daddy, I'm sorry!" My response is, "I don't want you to be just sorry, I want you to change your behaviour."

It is quite possible to have emotional regret, but not be willing to change. Scripture says this of Judas after he betrayed the Lord Jesus (Matt. 27:1-3). He was sorry for what he had done, but there was no change in his life. Sorrow without repentance only produces condemnation and condemnation led to his suicide. Scripture also says that Esau wept bitterly to regain the birthright which he sold to his brother, but there was no repentance in his character (Heb. 12:16-17).

The town drunk used to make an annual pilgrimage to a famous downtown church to be absolved of all his yearly sins. Stumbling down the aisle and weeping bitterly he would cry out, "Lord, forgive the cobwebs!" After seeing the ritual for numerous years the pastor became irritated at the empty repentance, and so as the man came forward the pastor prayed out loud, "Lord, forgive the cobwebs, but kill the spider!" Repentance is not just being sorry, but actually turning around in our behaviour. I am not suggesting that repentance is not deeply felt, for it is, but the source of repentance is in the will and not in our emotions. It is a firm resolve that since God is both for us and in us, we will change our behaviour.

John's message of repentance is that we should make a straight pathway for the coming of our Lord (Matt. 3:2-3). The entrance way of our life must be made straight for Christ to enter in his fullness. If there are corners, obstacles, ditches in our entrance way (things which we have not removed by repentance) then it takes a long time for Christ to overcome these obstacles and be Lord of our life. If you have invited Christ into your life, but you have not repented (e.g., forgiven the people who have hurt you, made restitution for things stolen or people cheated, confessed lies that you have told to others and about others), if you have not surrendered your own self-government, or given up the financial controls of your life, if you have not ceased in your judging of people and your holding of grudges, how can the Lord get into your life? Your foundation is inadequate and you will constantly be going over the same ground with him. Jesus says, "Do you want me to come in?" You reply, "Yes!" Then Jesus says, "Repent of your sins." Repentance clears the stage for Christ's Lordship and smooths out the rough places.

What valleys in your own life need to be lifted up? Do you need to repent of self-pity, a wrong assessment of yourself as a sick, depressed, ungifted member of the body of Christ? What hill needs to be leveled? Do you need to repent of such insecurity and ego presence that you require constant strokes to feel wanted? The pathway in each of our lives must be made straight for Jesus and likewise the pathway of the Canadian church must be made straight for Christ to bring the revival he desires.

As John was baptizing, many Pharisees and Sadducees came to him. No doubt these religious leaders did this in order to subvert the radical demands that John was making. Join the group and modify the standards! Many religious Canadians find no problem at all with repentance, it's just part of their accepted ritual. Repentance is just a few words ("Lord, I'm sorry") or a few symbols (show up on Sunday morning and bring your tithe in hand). But as John refused the shallow tokenism of the Pharisees and Sadducees, likewise we should refuse the same today.

Repentance is observable, not just words and symbols. Repentance is fruit which is grown on a healthy tree. Repentance is not the tree but the fruit of the tree. Do non-Christians know that you are a believer because of symbols or because of genuine repentance in your life? Is it words they hear or lifestyle they observe? Repentance is forsaking sin in order to participate in a new order called the Kingdom of Heaven. If you want to stay in the old order and sing the praise of the new, then you have not repented. If you have not made a radical break with your past, then you have not repented. If you have believed the gospel, yet are not obeying Jesus Christ as Lord, then you have not repented. Repentance is the first thing you must do if the Lord Jesus Christ is to come fully into you life. It is also the first thing that Canadians must do if Christ is to come fully alive in the church in our country.

If you have believed the gospel and not repented, then there are a number of side effects. You will become a miserable Christian. You will be bored, depressed, ineffective as a witness, constantly in trouble with someone, unsure if your prayers are being heard, discontented with the church you are in and occupying yourself with a thousand other things than the kingdom of God. You are a member of a carnal and comatose church which is ineffective in your community.

But if you have repented, turned around, Christ's presence is greater than before. Areas of conflict now become areas of growth and the Kingdom is no longer a threat but a challenge. Repentance will surely produce from observers the comment that "you are different."

Sincere returning to God causes God's own posture of judgment toward us to change (Joel 2:13-14). As we repent of our sin, God repents of his conclusion that we are to be disciplined or to miss out on his fullest blessing. Judgment by God in this context, is conditional upon man's response. God does not change, yet his judgments may or may not change according to our response or lack of it. Surely the word to the Ephesian church is a good example (Rev. 2:1-11). Although they were industrious in their activity and orthodox in their beliefs, their love for Jesus Christ had grown cold. Such a condition called for repentance with the threat of losing their witness if they did not respond. The absence of that church today suggests that the warning was not heeded. Jesus' words of assurance about the triumph of his church will need to be weighted by the obedience of that same church (Matt. 16:18).

What sin hinders your church from returning to the Lord? Is it loss of your first love? The tolerance of heretical teachers and immoral behaviour (Rev. 2:12-17)? The self-righteousness that claims nothing is wrong and therefore no need of repentance (1 John 1:8-10)? Have speech sins so polluted your church that the Holy Spirit has been grieved (Eph. 4:25-32)? Is there theft (Acts 5:1-11) or division in the fellowship (1 Cor. 1:10-17)? Have you resisted the leadership of the Holy Spirit as he reveals himself in gifted people (1Thess. 5:18-20)? Whatever it is, it needs cleansing through repentance before God can pour out his blessing (Joel 2:14).

PUBLIC REPENTANCE

Fortnightly, I meet with a group of pastors to pray for revival in Canada. Recently, the Lord led us to publish a statement of repentance in our major daily newspaper. We wrestled for many weeks over the wording of the statement, but our major controversy in drafting was whether or not we should publicly acknowledge our repentance. One argument said that the church was already perceived so badly, why add to this image? And yet we all knew God was asking us to acknowledge our shortcomings and only through this could others identify with us. I have enclosed this statement as an example of the specific nature of public repentance:

> "Whereas Canada is founded upon principles that recognize the supremacy of God and the rule of law:" Constitution Act, 1982)
>
> WE THE UNDERSIGNED, understanding these to be times of crisis, invite all people of goodwill to join us as we humble ourselves before God, repent and seek his face for mercy upon our land.
>
> 1. WE REPENT for failing to obey the biblical command to pray "for our leaders and legislators and for all who have authority over us." We commit ourselves to intercede that we may live "peaceful and quiet lives in godliness and honesty." 1 Timothy 2:2
>
> 2. WE REPENT for allowing our false self-confidence to confuse the clear proclamation that "there is one God and one mediator between God and men, the Man Christ Jesus ... who wants all men to be saved and to come to the knowledge of the truth." 1 Tim. 2:4, 5 We affirm that true

human worth and love derive from God who made man in His image.

3. WE REPENT of our involvement in the breakdown of family life by divorce, and the consequent suffering of our children. We commit ourselves to loving family life and the care of the parentless and single parents.

4. WE REPENT of slacking in our private responsibilities to take initiative in showing compassion for the poor and disadvantaged, "this was the sin of Sodom, she was arrogant, over-fed and unconcerned; they did not help the poor and needy." Ezekiel 16:49

5. WE REPENT of our greed and materialism of which chronic management-labour strife, our ever increasing national debt, and government operated lotteries are symbols. We commit ourselves to seek first the kingdom of God while believing His promise to "give us this day our daily bread." Matthew 6:3

6. WE REPENT of our inactivity in the face of the decreasing value of human life. We shudder when 70,000 babies a year have their lives violently taken from them: a legal abortion every 6 minutes. Psalm 139:13-16

7. WE REPENT of our sexual immorality that is leading us to a flood of pornography, the alarming rise of prostitution, child abuse, homosexuality, incest and rape. We commit ourselves with compassion and intelligent concern to work for private and public moral purity and the subsequent safety of children, women, and men.

8. WE REPENT of racial and cultural discrimination including anti-Semitism, which debase human dignity. We commit ourselves to respect the God-given worth of all people.

9. WE REPENT of allowing the fear of nuclear war to paralyze our hope for the future, and to confuse the issues of righteous peace. We commit ourselves to obey the words of Jesus Christ who as Prince of Peace says "FEAR NOT" and "BLESSED ARE THE PEACEMAKERS." We look for His return as King of Kings. Matthew 10:28; 2 Peter 3:10-13

WE ENCOURAGE you to participate in the renewal of

your local church through prayer, attendance and involvement. History reveals that in times of national repentance, God has withheld judgment and has shown loving kindness and mercy, even so we pray "GOD KEEP OUR LAND GLORIOUS AND FREE, O CANADA WE STAND ON GUARD FOR THEE."

PETITIONARY PRAYER

With the devastation everywhere, followed by a period of humility before God, Joel now instructs in the petitionary prayer to be given (2:17). "Spare Thy people, O Lord, and do not make thine inheritance a reproach, a byword among the nation. Why should they among the peoples say, 'Where is their God?' "

This is a verse that Canadians need to star, memorize, chant and pray. It is a petition inspired by God and thus a prayer we can be assured God wants to answer. "Spare your church in Canada, O Lord, and do not make us a reproach before the evil people of this nation. Why should they be allowed their mocking, 'Show us your God' when You alone rule this universe?"

IT'S BEGINNING TO RAIN

The sanctification after defeat now turns to be a sanctification before great victory. God is moved in pity for his people. Emotionally he is moved by their repentance, so much so that he is now zealous to deliver them from their painful and embarrassing position (2:18). Three things occur as a result of his activity.

First, he *restores the lost years* which the locusts have eaten (2:25). The restoration comes through a superabundant harvest, the threshing floors full of grain and the vats overflowing with oil and wine (2:24). How will this all come about, especially to a dry and parched land? God will restore the rainy season once again (2:23). Both early and late rains will mark the boundaries of God's climatic blessing. And why will God intervene in such a way? His concern is that his people would not be put to shame in the eyes of unbelievers (2:26-27). When we start to worry about the shame we have brought to God's name by our sin (Joshua 7:9), then God begins to worry about our name as it is being trampled by the enemy.

As a youth I was raised in Texas. It is not uncommon in that part of the United States to be able to smell rain showers approaching.

Sometimes you can see a cloud on the horizon and although it is many miles away you can smell the showers as they draw closer and closer. I think the same can be said for the rain showers of revival. Many of you, like myself, have been smelling the climatic change over the past few years in Canada. We know revival is coming, but we don't know what, if anything, we can do about it.

Joel's words give us some help. Have we seen and experienced the devastation (1:4-7; 2:1-11)? Have we taken the measured steps to humble ourselves in repentance (1:8-20; 2:12-17)? If these steps have been completed, we can look to God for the restoration of the rain and a superabundant harvest (2:21-27). The conviction of this process has led our own pastoral team to believe God for a one-hundred percent increase of new believers to our fellowship within the next year. We are asking every adult believer to win one person to Christ this year. The stage is being set now with deep repentance and humility before God. The watchword of the Azusa Street revival has become our own: "The depth of revival will be determined exactly by the depth of the spirit of repentance."[3]

Second, when God turns in zeal for his people *he pours out his Spirit* upon them (2:28-32). This scripture which was announced and demonstrated on the day of Pentecost (Acts 2:17-21) is a continual promise anytime God begins renewing his people. It is always applicable when the dark assault of the enemy has convinced us that we are drawing close to the day of the Lord (1:15; 2:1, 11, 31; 3:14). This prophecy was fulfilled at Pentecost and is being fulfilled repeatedly in church history and will have a last great fulfillment just before Jesus Christ comes again. Its fulfillment registers in our hearts the conviction that Jesus is coming back soon to gather his church and to judge the world.

It is estimated that since the Azusa Street revival of 1905-6, which was sparked by the Welsh revival under Evan Roberts, over one million people per year have joined the ranks of Pentecostal denominations. The charismatic renewal of the past twenty-five years has also swollen these ranks. However, I believe there is a revival coming which will be greater than these two previous waves. But the cost of such a work will not be less than the ones before, the cost so clearly spelled out by Joel.

Third, the *Lord draws near in judgment* for all the nations of the world (3:1-17). God's wrath will be unfurled against those who have mistreated his own people and each person will be called into that dreadful valley of decision, either to call upon the name of the Lord and be saved, or be destroyed as the enemy of God. Such certainty of the eventual judgment of every person is not only grounds for personal reassesment, but also for warning others of impending danger. The heart convicting cry that Jesus Christ will come again to judge the living and the dead, has lost its cutting edge in Canada. Only heaven-sent revival will quicken once again that message.

RESPOND, DON'T JUST SIT THERE

What will you do with this message from Joel? Is God calling you to a ministry of tears for the broken state of your own life and the Canadian church? If so, begin to weep.

Is God calling you to halt some normal activity and to devote your time to fasting and prayer for Canada? Are you called repeatedly to cry out, "Spare your people, O Lord"?

Is God calling you to rend your own heart before him? To acknowledge and repent of all lingering sin?

You may not be able to do much, but do what you can. Just passing through this section will not help you; it will only harden your heart if you do not make some gesture of response. Locusts are eating up the land and the people are starving. Is it not your turn to step in and do something about it?

1   see Theodore Lactsch, *The Minor Prophets* (St. Louis: Concordia Publishing House, 1956) p. 114-119.
2   as quoted in Kenneth A. Berven, "gluttony," *Again* (Vol. 6, No. 3).
3   Frank Bartleman, *Azusa Street* (Plainfield, New Jersey: Logos International, 1980) p. 9.

Chapter 7

THE POWER IN REVIVAL

The Canadian journalist Peter Newman was in New Brunswick on one of his first assignments and began making small talk with a farmer. "Have you lived here all your life?" he inquired. The farmer thought for a moment and replied, "No, not yet."

What Newman had expected was a reflection of the man's past, but what he got was an answer looking towards the future. Canadian Christians need to adopt a similar attitude towards the Holy Spirit who is the power in revival. Whether we are kosher evangelicals who quote 1 Corinthians 12:13 or rigid pentecostals and quote Acts 2:4, both of us need to admit that there is so much more to know of the Holy Spirit than is presently understood by either group.

In any new discovery of the Holy Spirit, it is necessary that we know the platoe of orthodoxy, the right and proper platform for the Holy Spirit, and also the edges that descend into heterodoxy. In one section of Jesus' upper room discourse we are given that necessary information (John 14:1-31).

MODELING JESUS

At the beginning and end of this section, Jesus addresses the problem of fear. The first word chosen by John to record this message is *tarasso* (v.1), to be frightened, stirred up, disturbed, or thrown into confusion. The second word is *deiliato* (v.27). We are most familiar with this word as Paul uses it to exhort Timothy not to be cowardly or timid (2 Tim. 1:7).

Can you identify with these feelings of fright and timidity? Jesus could. Three times before he utters these words of comfort, he himself is disquieted. At the death of his friend Lazarus, Jesus is deeply moved in spirit and troubled (John 11:33). Later he confesses to his Father, "My soul has become troubled; and what shall I say, Father, save me from this hour? But for this purpose I came to this hour" (John 12:27). At the last supper Jesus was again troubled in his spirit and said, "Truly, truly I say to you, that one of you will betray me" (John 13:21).

How is it possible for Jesus to say to his disciples, "let not your hearts be troubled" (14:1) if he himself was troubled? The answer is that in every instance where Jesus was troubled, confused or even drawn toward cowardice, God the Father drew close to him and led him through that disturbance.

He was so close to Jesus at the tomb of Lazarus that Jesus could thank Him that he always heard his prayer (11:41-42). When he was troubled over his purpose in life, an affirming voice came out of heaven so loud that the people were able to hear it: "Father, glorify thy name".... "I have both glorified it and will glorify it again" (John 12:28). Even when he was betrayed by Judas he had the courage to dismiss him quickly (John 13:27).

In these experiences our Lord learned that when he was troubled or confused to lean upon the Father who was always close by. He therefore models for us what it means to depend upon another for strength. Using his relationship with the Father as a paradigm, Jesus reveals how his own disciples can now be aided in their stations of trouble. Although he is going to be with the Father, he is going to give his disciples another Comforter (John 14:17) and if his disciples rely upon that Comforter, as he did upon his Father, then they shall navigate through fear, confusion and even timidity.

GOD THE SPIRIT

Who is this Comforter that we are to trust? He is God! He is God! He is God!

In the words of the Nicene Creed, "He proceeds from the Father and Son, and who with the Father and Son is to be worshipped and glorified." Why? Because he is God!

His titles display his diety. The Holy Spirit is called the Spirit of God (Matt. 3:16), the Spirit of the Lord (Luke 4:18), the Spirit of

Christ (Rom. 8:9), the Spirit of God's Son (Gal. 4:6), the Eternal Spirit (Heb. 9:14) and it is in his name along with the Father and Son that we are baptized (Matt. 28:19).

This Comforter is not *heteros paraklatos*, a Comforter of a substance different from the Father and the Son, but he is *allon paraklaton*, another of the same substance of the Father and the Son. He is God!

"Jewish monotheism," says William Hendricksen, "refuses to accept the possibility that divine essence can unfold itself in more than one person."[1] Today it appears that some Canadians refuse to accept the possibility that divine essence can unfold itself in more than two persons. Surely it is heresy to be a pneumatic unitarian and worship exclusively the Holy Spirit. So also is it to be binatarian, one who worships only the Father and Son. The plateau of orthodoxy demands that we honor as God the Father, the Son, and the Holy Spirit.

Let me hasten to add that there is no text in scripture which calls us to worship and glorify the Holy Spirit. The statement of the Nicene Creed is a deduction based upon his diety: if he is then he is to be worshipped and glorified.

Are we not in need of repentance for cheapening the Holy Spirit and by treating him as a messenger angel rather than a divine person? The Godhead functions in a tandem relationship and we are not to divide up the Trinity according to those who are deserving or less deserving, those of honor and those of less honor. But with equality, we are to glorify the Father, because of the work of the Son, through the power of the Holy Spirit. This is orthodoxy in the Holy Spirit and the power for revival.

DISCLOSURE BY THE HOLY SPIRIT

The Gospel formula in Acts calls us to believe in the Lord Jesus Christ and to receive the Holy Spirit (Acts 2:38). In our evangelistic presentations we speak of "receiving Christ," but the weight of the biblical data suggests that we are called to believe in Christ and receive his Spirit. Christ is seated with the Father in heaven, but he dispenses himself to believers by means of the Holy Spirit. In John's language, the ascended Lord was to give the Comforter to be with believers and to be in the believer (14:17). By the means of this indwelling he himself would be disclosed to the believer.

Jesus went on to say, "He who has my commandments, and keeps them, he it is who loves me; and he who loves me shall be loved by my Father, and I will love him, and will disclose myself to him (John 14:21)." But what is the nature of this disclosure? Is it conversion that Jesus has in mind, or is it part of the sanctification process? The conversion side says, "the verb is aoristic (similar to past tense) and is parallel to the statement of the Father and Son making their abode with the believer (14:23), therefore it must be conversion." The sanctification side says, "Keeping the commandments is no way to become a Christian, he must be talking about subsequent disclosures to believers."

And so the "got it all" group squares off with the "something more" group and they write books back and forth at one another and preach sermons against each other.

What I want to suggest is that both are correct and that orthodoxy demands both. Paul in his epistle to the Ephesians assures us that every believer has been blessed with every spiritual blessing in heavenly places (Eph. 1:13-14). We have received the pledge of our inheritance, the Holy Spirit. Since the Holy Spirit is a person and not an influence, you cannot get more or less of him. You either have him or you don't. In one sense there is no need for a second blessing; the first is sufficient for every person for all time.

But the "got it all" Paul, in his very next breath utters what appears to be a "something moreism." He prays that they might be given a "Spirit of wisdom and of revelation in the knowledge of him, that the eyes of your hearts might be enlightened, so that you might know the hope of his calling and the riches of his inheritance in the saints and the surpassing greatness of his power towards us who believe" (Eph. 1:17-19). He seems to be saying that coming to Christ is one thing, but comprehending all that has transpired in our coming to him is another. It will take some time for us to unwrap and comprehend all that is contained in the gift of salvation.

PERSONAL TESTIMONY

On November 4, 1964 I knelt as a student in my dormitory room and received Jesus Christ as my Saviour. That evening I was both baptized by the Spirit into the body of Christ and inundated by the presence of the Holy Spirit (1 Cor. 12:13). The teaching I received as a new Christian was exceptional. I was soon, however, taught that knowledge was more important than the Spirit. No one ever said this directly, but the emphasis lent that interpretation. I was immediately taught all the things that the Spirit could not do or would not do during this age. At one point I was even shooed away from a Keswick conference lest I be confused in my thinking about the Holy Spirit.

This theology of the Spirit did me well for some ten years. Then my Christian life began to dry up. I ventured into a severe crisis of faith regarding the nature of prayer. It appeared to me that prayer was of little value because I never saw any direct results of these prayers. This led me into a period of deep agnosticism and because of this drought I am capable today of empathizing with evangelicals who are actually practising agnostics. They know the gospel is true and that Christ was very real in their life at one point, but now spiritual reality appears vague and far away.

As I analyzed my dilemma I was convinced of two things. First, "got it all" theology left me dry, but "something more" theology bordered on being a Galatian heresy.

Consulting one of the standard works of the Holy Spirit I was led to reinvestigate the old formula, "grieve not, quench not, be filled with, and walk in."[2] As I reflected on this formula I found it to be quite correct, only the perimeters needed to be expanded. The Holy Spirit was to be viewed as God and not depreciated as something less. I was forced back to my conversion, this time to slowly unwrap every spiritual blessing that had been given to me in Christ. What I discovered was that the Holy Spirit had been there all along in my life, only waiting for me to acknowledge his presence and give him an opportunity to direct my life. The way for him to be real in my life was the same way he was real on November 4, 1964; by the grace of God through faith.

The re-emergence of the Holy Spirit in my life was slow and quiet and spread out over two years. For my wife and many of my friends it was sudden, critical, and sensationally transforming. But I knew that the Holy Spirit had begun to do some new things in my life. I then realized that walking in the Spirit was the process of continually turning myself over to the Spirit in obedience and continually beholding the face of the Lord (John 14:21; Eph. 5:18; 2 Cor. 3:18). As I began to take these steps, Jesus Christ was revealed to me more and more by the Holy Spirit.

Through this whole procedure I only had to lay aside one exegetical conviction, namely that certain gifts of the Holy Spirit had ceased. Slowly I began to admit that God could give to the church today any gifts of the Spirit he desired.[3]

Today my "something more" friends believe that I have been "baptized in the Holy Spirit." My "got it all" friends believe that I have been "filled with the Holy Spirit." My "something more" friends don't think I have gone far enough in my theology while my "got it all" friends think I have gone too far. Quite frankly, I think I am just being orthodox in my theology and my experience.

In his fanciful journey to heaven, C.S. Lewis suggests that there we will not be free to be dry.[4] In heaven, we will not have the choice to be empty, cerebral, quenching Christians. Our only choice will be to be filled with the Spirit. But on earth, it is our choice to be filled with the Spirit. It is optional whether or not we will unwrap all that has been given to us in salvation, to drink deeply of the wells of salvation.

Many evangelicals suspect that movement toward the Spirit-filled life is "something more" theology which requires they repudiate their "got it all" theology. But this is not true. The call is to claim and act upon all that we possessed in Christ, when we believed in him and received his Spirit. It is the straight line of grace and faith that runs to the foot of the cross that will allow the fulness of the Holy Spirit. We must not let the "frozen chosen" keep us from the fulness of the Spirit nor fear of the "lunatic fringe" prohibit us from having all that is ours in Christ.

A.W. Tozer encouraged Christians in this direction with these four simple principles. "You will have nothing unless you go after it." We must be persistent in our unwrapping all that has been given to us in salvation. "You may have as much as you insist on having." We need to specifically ask God to fill us with his Holy Spirit (Luke 11:14; Eph. 5:18). "You will have as little as you are satisfied with." If you are satisfied with the unwrappings thus far, there will be no more for you. "You now have as much as you really want." What you have is what you have asked for and if you are asking for no more, then there is no more for you.[5]

CHARACTER AND THE WORKS OF THE SPIRIT

Another imagined polarity is between the fruit of the Spirit and the gifts of the Spirit. Is character more important than gifts or do we overlook minor flaws for the prospect of great spiritual giftedness?

Orthodoxy accentuates both. Jesus said, "If you love me, you will keep my commandments" (14:15). But he also said, "He who believes in me, the works that I do shall he do also; and greater works than these shall he do; because I go to the Father" (14:12). Orthodoxy demands both purity and obedience in our life, but it is to be matched with great spiritual giftedness. Because Jesus has gone to the Father and has sent the Comforter to us, he says that we who believe in him will do greater works than he did on earth. Before we look at this promise more closely, let me relay an experience that happened on our trip across Canada.

We sat down for tea one evening in a delightful home. The owner was a successful lawyer and had just given the evening message on spiritual gifts in his home church. He asked for a candid appraisal of his message and assured me that I would not hurt his feelings by anything I said.

After a few honest words of appreciation I said, "I see three problems with what you said tonight. First, only one-half of your audience can exercise these gifts (women were forbidden to speak publicly in the meeting). Second, you have no structures for these gifts to be exercised. And last, your list of spiritual gifts acknowledges only A-P exist, while Q-Z have passed away."

As you can imagine this provided fuel for several hours of conversation. He relished in his apologetic as he recounted the historical and biblical arguments against healing and other controversial gifts.

The next morning I found myself in the pastor's study of a large university church in the same city. My first question was the same I had asked in almost every interview conducted on that trip. "What is the most significant thing you have seen in your church in the last two years?" Without hesitation the pastor replied, "It was the healing of that blind woman last year!"

I jumped in my chair. "What blind woman?" For the next few minutes he described the complete healing of a woman who had diabetic blindness for five years. She had come to special services convinced that the pastor was to pray for her recovery. This he did for five successive nights with no results. The meetings ended and she returned to her remote home in the same condition she had come.

However, the next morning she was able to see her three children for the first time in five years. She immediately drove to the pastor's home and bore witness to the miracle of healing. In my file cabinet there is a full-page newspaper clipping from her home-town paper recording this event.

As I reflected on this experience I was amazed by the contrast I had heard in less than twenty-four hours. One moment there was a wholesale rejection of healing, and in the next there was an empirical and heart-moving testimony suggesting that God is still in the business of doing marvelous things.

The first man was a member of my own Bible-believing tradition and my sympathies were naturally with him. The second pastor was in a "liberal" tradition and less "charismatic" than I thought he should be. But it was with the second I had to rest my case.

Some believe that the works of John 14:12 are exclusively evangelistic in nature. It is said that the breadth of our evangelistic opportunities would be greater than the Lord possessed in Israel. It is true that the work of God is that we would believe in him who has been sent (John 6:29).

However, we cannot get away from the fact that on the majority of occasions where works (*ergos*) is used, it does so of divine manifestations which demonstrate the power of the proclaimed word. The abiding presence of Christ through the Holy Spirit will thus enhance a verbal proclamation and a demonstration of the power of God. Orthodoxy demands fruitful obedience to the Spirit, coupled with the power of God.

BURNT, BUT STILL WILLING

Several years ago I was leaving a church building when I was met by one of my former parishioners. I stuck out my hand for the usual greeting, he doing the same, only with some hesitation in his eye. As I gripped his hand it erupted in mine. Across the palm of his hand was a blister from a burn and unconsciously he allowed me to shake his injured hand. As you can well imagine, I was very careful about shaking hands for some time after that event.

Many Christians reveal the same hesitation about the ministry of the Holy Spirit. With the growth of pentecostal churches and the emergence of the charismatic movement, many have had bad and unfortunate experiences with those who claim to be empowered by the Holy Spirit. However, for those who have been burnt and are still willing to grow in the knowledge of the Holy Spirit, the encouragement of the upper room discourse is helpful: confess that the Holy Spirit is God; lean on the assistance of the Spirit as Jesus leaned on the Father; by grace and faith unwrap all that was given to you in the gift of salvation; expect that Jesus will alter your character and gift you for ministry by the work of the Holy Spirit. Don't grieve the Spirit (Eph. 4:30). Don't quench the Spirit (1 Thess. 5:19). Keep on being filled with the Spirit (Eph. 5:18). Surely this is the only power we have to see Canada awakened for Jesus Christ.

1   William Hendricksen, *New Testament Commentary: Exposition of the Gospel According to John*, (Grand Rapids: Baker Book House, 1972) p.271.
2   Lewis Sperry Chafer, *He That is Spiritual*, (Grand Rapids: Zondervan, 1969)
3   George Mallone, *Those Controversial Gifts*, (Downers Grove: Inter-Varsity Press, 1983).
4   C.S. Lewis, *The Great Divorce*, (New York: The MacMillan Company, 1967) p.44.
5   A.W. Tozer, *The Incredible Christian*, (Harrisburg: Christian Publications, Inc., 1964) pp.62-64.

Chapter 8

POWER EVANGELISM

In December 1973 I was scheduled to speak to a group of Christian professional women at an evangelistic dinner party. The day before the dinner I developed a severe case of laryngitis. After drafting a close friend to bail me out if worse came to worst, I choked down a quart of "Granny Greensprings" and spent the afternoon before the party sleeping. While I was asleep a very distinct picture came to my mind: I dreamed that I was surrounded in a white jacket much like those used to restrain psychiatric patients. Awaking from my sleep, I thought I was uncomfortable because of my bulky sweater; so I took it off and went back to sleep. A second time I had the same vivid picture in my mind. I awoke again, this time removing the comforter from my bed. A third time this very vivid picture came to mind while I slept, but when I awoke this time the Lord clearly gave me the interpretation for the picture which I had been seeing. He said to me, "You are surrounded in my love, and you are surrounded in my grace." The word was so profound I fell back on the bed in amazement. Sensing that God was speaking and giving direction for the evening, I dressed and went to the dinner party. While driving into the city, I spoke to the Lord about the dream. Unsure whether the dream was just for me or for someone else, I told him that I was prepared to share it with anyone who could be helped by it.

There were over five hundred women present when I arrived. We went through the formalities of eating and the Christmas program. At last it came my turn to speak. I strapped a microphone close to my mouth and began. But just a few minutes into the presentation the Lord seemed to lay upon me the necessity of sharing what had happened that afternoon. As I came to the word, "You are surrounded in my love and in my grace," the Lord powerfully converted a woman, a Jehovah's Witness, sitting only three rows from me. As with Lydia (Acts 16:14), God opened her heart and filled her with his grace. Crying later that evening, she told me that it was not just the gospel message that softened her heart, but the intimate communication that God gave to her through the dream. It had opened her eyes to receive all Christ had done for her at Calvary. Through a gift of prophecy, this time through a dream, God spoke his dynamic word to this new sister.

This little incident highlights the theme of this chapter, the release of spiritual gifts as they are used in evangelism. My conviction is that Canadian revival will see the use of this combination and hence our need to be knowledgeable about it. The ideas in this chapter actually originated in a course taught at Fuller Seminary by John Wimber and Peter Wagner, *Signs and Wonders and Church Growth* (MC510), although my theological sympathies have been in this direction for some time and my pastoral experience is proving the same to be true.

The thesis is quite simple. "Program evangelism, that is the presentation of the Gospel which attempts to reach the natural mind by rational means alone (e.g., crusades, debates, lectures) is not sufficient" to reach Canada for Christ.[1] "What is needed today is power evangelism, a presentation of the gospel which is rational, but also transcends the rational. It is a proclamation which demonstrates the power of God through signs and wonders and introduces people to the manifest presence of God."

TO CEASE OR NOT TO CEASE, THAT IS THE QUESTION?

One of the great tragedies to befall the evangelical church in North America is the notion that certain gifts of the Holy Spirit ceased with the death of Apostles and the completion of the canon, most notable the gifts mentioned in 1 Corinthians 12:8-11. This strong reaction to gifts caused me to write what I believe is a sensible approach to the subject in a book called *Those Controversial Gifts*. The response I have had to its publication, especially from evangelicals who formerly disagreed with me but are now changing their minds, confirms that this perspective has not only stifled the growth of believers but also hindered the expansion of the church through evangelism.

The tradition that I came from argued that the gifts of the Spirit ceased with the canonization of Scripture. The proof for that position was found in 1 Corinthians 13:10, "But when the perfect comes the partial shall be done away." This defense has infected thousands of Canadian churchmen over the years and is a block to a power move of the Holy Spirit.

However, any serious exegesis of that verse will not stand such an interpretation. There is nothing in the Greek word for "perfect" that denotes Scripture. There is nothing in the context to suggest Scripture, nor anything in the grammar to force us to conclude Paul is referring to Scripture. I challenge those who argue such a position, to produce one major commentary on Corinthians that articulates this position. If they are not to be found, why in heaven's name have we lived under this oppressive assumption? I think there are three reasons.

First, there is *carnality*. The carnal mind, which all of us possess from time to time, wants to control God, to tell him what he can do and what he can't do. The carnal mind wants to systematize God in order that he won't disturb our creatureliness. The carnal mind wants to do ministry without the help of God, to disprove Jesus' word that "without me you can do nothing" (John 15:5). We believe that we can do ministry without the power of God; thus we rely instead upon our mastery of techniques, abilities and skills, hard work, the desire to be good and maintaining of theological orthodoxy. These are our sources of ministry, and in and of themselves they are carnal because they are not rooted in dependence upon Jesus Christ and the power of the Holy Spirit.

The second hindrance is *emotional fear*. We fear the presence and power of God. We squirm at a faith which is lived with more than the cognitive process (not less, but more). There are fears that the presence of God might cause us to lose control of ourselves (a no no for evangelicals), that we might be embarrassed by tears or confession of sin, and that we might do something with our body (e.g., raise hands, pray prostrate) which is unorthodox in our setting. We fear what people will think of us and begin to say about us. Fear of being out of step and looking foolish paralyze our walk. Killian O'Donnell, a Catholic theologian, has said; "The charismatic movement is not too emotional, it's too personal." I find this exactly the point. Evangelicals want a personal religion, but not a relationship with

God which threatens their emotional well-being.

Third, many have shut the door on spiritual gifts as a *reaction to a classical pentecostalism*. It is the outrageous things that have been done in the name of the Lord which have thrown many evangelicals off the track. One pentecostal healer, dying of alcoholism in a slum hotel, invites the response, "You see, I told you healing was of the devil." I once counselled a Calvinistic pastor, who was an alcoholic and eventually hung himself in the attic of his church. Does this mean John Calvin was of the devil? Goodness no! There will always be false prophets and carnal leaders within the camp of God's genuine workers. Many of my close friends, both reformed evangelicals and pentecostals, have seen all the abuses you could dream up, yet they still operate the gifts in the power of the Holy Spirit. To be filled with the Holy Spirit and to exercise all the gifts of the Spirit does not mean that you must adopt holas bolas a pentecostal framework or culture. It simply means that the Holy Spirit needs free reign in your life, ministry and congregation. He needs free, unchecked access to doing the work of Jesus.

POWER EVANGELISM

"Power evangelism is confronting an unbelieving world with the message of the gospel, in the power of the Holy Spirit, using the gifts of the Holy Spirit." As Paul said; "And my message and my preaching were not in persuasive words of wisdom, but in demonstration of the Spirit and power, that your faith should not rest on the wisdom of men, but on the power of God" (1 Cor. 2:4-5).

Consistently, people were amazed with the authority of Jesus' message (Luke 4:36). I assure you that it was not a homiletical device that the Gospel writers had in mind when they used this term "authority". It was the power of God, released to authenticate the message that captured their attention. It was proof that the Kingdom rule of God had invaded planet earth.

Let me quickly review for you some examples of power evangelism in the New Testament.

First, there was power through *praise and tongues* in Acts 2. The one hundred and twenty, when filled with the Holy Spirit, spoke the mighty deeds of God in a foreign dialect. Their funny Galilean accents, recognizable by all, were overcome by speech of a new language, languages known by the world-wide visitors to Jerusalem.

This, coupled with rapturous praise, and clear proclamation, saw the conversion of 3,000 people in one day. This is "transrational evangelism."

Second, power evangelism is seen in the use of *prophetic gifts*. Paul argues that when prophecy is used in the church, and at this point we need not merge teachers and prophets (Acts 13:1), the unbelievers will be convicted, have the secrets of their hearts revealed, and falling on their faces they will confess that God is among you (1 Cor. 14:24-25).

Such encounters happen often when genuine prophetic gifts are flowing. David Watson once relayed to me the story of a young girl in his church, who, after sitting through part of an evangelistic service, decided to leave. Realizing that she had forgotten her sweater, she returned to her pew just as a prophetic word was being spoken. The word was so accurate for her life, she knelt and received Jesus Christ as her Lord and Saviour. Such examples were multiplied in the days of the Jesus movement, and will again lead us in a Canadian revival.

Third, it is expressed through a *word of knowledge*. Jesus' own ministry to the woman at the well is a most fitting example here. The Father conveyed to the Son during this encounter that the woman had five husbands, and the one she had now was not her husband (John 4:17,29). Her response was not only to believe, but to bring her friends as well. Jesus' conversation with the woman set the stage for this power encounter and thus her conviction that Jesus was the Messiah. I have ministered with people this last year, and have even exercised this gift myself, who have led people to Christ through a word of knowledge along with their proclamation of the gospel.

Fourth, it is through the *discernment and deliverance of evil spirits* in people. Mary Magdalene, from whom Jesus drove out seven demons, became one of our Lord's chief followers (Luke 8:2).

Many Canadians have given the devil a foothold in their lives through occultish spirits and all other manners of perversion. Such people will not be reached through a rational proclamation alone. What is needed is the liberation from enslaving spirits by the power of God as the gospel is proclaimed. This ministry will no doubt be needed for believers as well, especially for those who have not dealt with repentance when they received Christ.

Fifth, it is active through the ministry of *healing*. One-fifth of the gospel accounts relate the ministry of healing by our Lord. The man with palsy is pronounced a twin blessing, forgiveness of sins and restoration to his physical body (Luke 5:24-26). The action brought astonishment, fear and glorification from the observers.

At a conference I attended several months ago, a similar experience transpired. The first night of the conference I observed sitting across from me a young girl, with her limp, paralyzed legs elevated in her wheel chair. The next morning she ran up to the platform to tell her incredible story. As a ballerina, she developed an unknown disease and was paralyzed in both legs for five years. The once muscular thighs and calfs, now looked starved from their lack of use. Pulling herself across the floor to the T.V. she heard the gospel message from a television evangelist. Restored in Spirit, for she had only been a believer for three months, she made her way to the conference. The night of the first meeting, several stayed behind to pray for her healing. The following morning was like seeing the lame man in the book of Acts, "Walking and leaping and praising God" (Acts 3:8). And much like in the gospels, the fear of God spread among the observers. Healing is the new strategy for household evangelism. In some cultures, if you win the father, the whole family will come to Christ. Now, if one member of a family is saved and healed, the message of good news runs throughout the whole family. Healing will be a major factor in this Canadian revival.

Sixth, through *visions*. Peter's vision of the descending sheet of unclean animals, and the preparatory vision given to Cornelius, all play their part in Peter's proclamation to this Gentile and his subsequent conversion with his household (Acts 10). The story I told at the beginning of this chapter, suggests that such visions (this time through a dream) still occur and will be used of God to win the lost.

Seventh, through the *raising of the dead*. In Jesus' raising of Lazarus, many Jews believed in him (John 11:45). Through Peter's raising of the dead Dorcas, the entire city of Joppa heard the word and believed (Acts 9:36-43).

By the testimony of a third-world evangelist, one which I heard only a few weeks ago, the dead are being prayed over and raised to the glory of God. This evangelist was used to raise a little girl who had been dead for about eight hours. She is known to everyone because she is now the sister-in-law of the evangelist, he met and married her older sister in the process.

Do we stop preaching and just engage in signs and wonders? No! Fourteen times in Acts there is the correlation between preaching and signs and wonders. We do both. The message of the Kingdom both heard and seen is the only thing that can convince a secular and skeptical Canadian public.

Jesus commissioned the apostles with authority to heal the sick and cast out demons (Matt. 10:1-15). He also gave that authority to non-apostles, such as the seventy (Luke 10:1-20), Phillip in Samaria (Acts 8:5-8), and some unnamed people (Luke 9:49). Although we may not see ourselves as having the same authority as the original twelve, surely we can see ourselves among these others. Ordinary people, controlled by the Holy Spirit and useful vehicles to communicate Jesus' words and works.

GIFTS: HOW THEY OPERATE?

The reception and use of spiritual gifts should be viewed as dynamic rather than static. The static view of gifts says that they are our property which we get when we come to Christ, each having at least one, or two or three at the most. A fluid view of gifts suggests that a believer does not possess gifts, but receives gifts from God to be used at special times and occasions. In this view, in evangelistic undertakings, it is possible for a believer to have access to all the gifts of the spirit, if they should need them. If we have the Spirit, then we have access to all the Spirit's tools, and he will dispense such tools as he sees fit. Prophecy is a case in point. Jeremiah 31:33-34 predicts the prophetic potential of all believers. The fulfillment of this word is seen at Pentecost (Acts 2:17) and in Paul's clear suggestion that all can prophesy (1 Cor. 14:24,31) in an orderly manner.

The fluid view of gifts causes trouble for some because they fail to grasp the stages in gift development. Peter Wagner sees this development in four steps.[2]

First, gifts are perceived as a *role*. "The doing of the acts which you see occurring in scripture, by means of your natural ability, to the degree that you are able (rational)." I am called to help, give financially, share Christ with others and to pray for the sick, irrespective of any gifting. I do these things out of obedience to Jesus Christ, because he has called me to do so.

Second, gifts can be seen as *anointings* or as *gracelets*. Occasionally, there will be a "manifestation of a gift as ordained by God (transrational)." As you minister in an area of obedience (role) you will find God often anointing you with a special capacity to do what is needed. There may be an abundance in giving or power to actually see a person healed for whom you have prayed.

Third, there are *ministries*. The increase of the occasion, use and dimensions of the gracelets means that you have a specific ministry in this area. Repetition in the anointing is a ministry call and growth in the area will take place as you take opportunity to exercise your anointing.

Last, is the gift as an *office*. The appointment made by God through repeated anointings and maturity is now recognized by the church. The body acknowledges that God has set you apart to this function.

What this development allows is a view of gifts whereby the Holy Spirit is truly in charge. I personally expect to exercise all the gifts of the Spirit (as role and gracelet) when needed in obedience to Christ. This will not cause me to value others less, as though I am sufficient in and of myself. Because I may have an occasional gracelet in an area, does not mean I have a ministry in that area. My need of others, like Paul's appeal in 1 Corinthians 12, is the need for others at the level of ministry and office.

Most Christians are at level one (roles) to greater and lesser degrees of effectiveness. The jump to ministry and office is so formidable, something it is thought that only full-time clergy can achieve, that they fail to attempt anything. Gift development is taught best when concentration is placed at level two (gracelet/ anointing). How do I learn to hear Jesus speak to me through the Holy Spirit? How do I know his directives for sharing with non-Christians? What can I do in order to develop the frequency of anointing in a particular area?

Persuasive words, slick programs and charming personalities will not win Canada to Christ. Paul's reliance upon preaching Christ crucified in the power and demonstration of the Holy Spirit, this is our only hope (1 Cor. 2:1-5). Some will say that I am calling for a "pentecostal revival." If you mean the culture and theology of classical pentecostalism, as we see it in Canada today, the answer is no! Pentecostals are in as much need as any other group in our country today. But if you mean, revival born in the outpouring of the Holy Spirit and accompanied by all the gifts the Spirit wants to impart, the answer is definitely yes! Evangelism needs power to be effective and there is only one source of power for the Christian.

1 Most of the Wimber material is recorded in his unpublished notes which are given to his students. Material from this notebook is in quotation marks without any further reference.
2 These suggestions are contained in the Wimber notes and Peter C. Wagner's, *Your Spiritual Gifts Can Help Your Church Grow* (Glendale, California: Regal, 1976)

Chapter 9

THAT THEY ALL MIGHT BE ONE

Recently I attended a lecture at which the Mennonite theologian John Howard Yoder spoke. He argued that the visible unity of the church was a pre-condition for credible mission to the world. The Canadian church by contrast, as we suggested in Chapter 3, is characterized by division. These divisions are so deep and have lasted so long, only a God-sent revival can alter this pattern.

THAT THE WORLD MIGHT BELIEVE

Why should we care about the unity of the church? Because Jesus prayed for it (John 17:20-23)! It is our Lord who set the agenda, not some religious bureaucrats in a far away country. His work on the cross has broken down the barriers which separated people (Eph. 4:1-6). The unity has already been given, it must now be obeyed and manifested. Although one may not agree with all the activities of the World Council of Churches, it is to be acknowledged that they have taken seriously this task. Evangelicals have chosen to isolate themselves not only from the World Council but also from one another. In a day in which "church growth" mania has invaded so many of our churches, are we not given by our Lord an agenda for proclamation and witness? Did he not say that if we were one the world would believe and know that God had sent his Son to save the world (John 17:21,23)? Surely this should be part of our strategy to reach the seventy percent of Canadians who do not follow Christ.

WHERE DO WE BEGIN?

Here are some suggestions on how this process can begin, suggestions that start with personal attitudes then reach out to corporate activities. Let me list for you steps for improving our personal attitude and behaviour with respect to unity, given by Juan Carlos Ortiz.

First, we must commit ourselves to *never speak against another pastor or church.* Do not attempt to inflate yourself by destroying the reputation of another believer.

Second, when you have been offended by another person or church, be prepared to *forgive seventy times seven,* a countless number of times (Matt. 18:21-35).

Third, *ignore all divisions.* Because someone was offended in the past and erected a barrier between you and another person or tradition, jump over those barriers and go to the heart of a new relationship. Old wounds should not hinder new beginnings.

Fourth, *pray with and for any Christian* God brings across your path. Public prayers need to be said in every church for the impact of the whole church on the city. Interpersonal prayer is also the fastest way to break down all barriers and to begin reconstruction of a new relationship.

UNITY PROPOSAL

Another proposal for a practical expression of unity comes from the Church renewal author, Howard Snyder.

> Whenever possible in cities around the world large public rallies should be held regularly, uniting in the city all the people of God who will cooperate. If in major cities around the world if all true Christians could unite regularly in a "great congregation" to joyfully sing to God, hear the Word, and bear witness, the impact would be incalculable. Such rallies would give public, visible testimony to the unity of the Body of Christ and put faith in the center of the public arena once more. These gatherings should be regular and frequent (probably once a month), and they should unite all who are willing to confess that Jesus Christ is Lord and Saviour whether Catholic or Protestant, or Orthodox. They should be held in large public arenas wherever possible. Here the church in each city could recover some sense

of peoplehood that would cross denominational and con-
fessional lines, and here the world would glimpse reality of
the unified church.[1]

To the average pastor or lay leader caught up in the day to day
details in denominational commitments, and well aware of local
ecumenical tensions, the above proposal for a united public witness
is just a wishful dream. The organizational details alone would be
overwhelming. Besides, there are enough difficulties trying not to
offend one's own congregation within, why risk offending members
with something one would have virtually no control over?

Evangelicals have often attempted intra-church unity through
evangelistic crusades, economic sharing and para-church works,
and pastoral fellowships. On some occasions these efforts have been
most fruitful. At other times, however, they have led to further
divisions and despair. Ministerials are often subtle battle grounds for
conflicting egos, and the wise pastor can always have a previous
engagement to cover his absence. Disheartened church leaders have
concluded that the results do not usually merit the effort.

At one time or another I had these feelings about intra-church
cooperation. However, in the last few years my perspective has
changed. Six years ago, half a dozen pastors in our city began to meet
fort-nightly. We were concerned about church renewal in our city
and nation. We had no grandiose schemes for bringing renewal, only
the conviction that we were to cooperate with one another in any
way possible. To focus our agenda we signed a written covenant
contracting ourselves to one another for one year. Gathering
together every other Wednesday morning for two hours, we worshipped, interceded for our city, and prayed for one another's needs.
Slowly the fellowship began to grow in dearness to our hearts. We
soon found ourselves doing everything possible not to miss the
meeting. We began to sense that we really needed one another and
that God was manifesting himself to us in those hours.

Although we came from a variety of denominational back-
grounds and doctrinal preferences (amillenialist and premillenialist,
real presence and mere symbol, sprinklers and immersers), we began
to sense that our primary identity was to be in the Father and in his
Son. Although our views of the Holy Spirit were quite different we
were committed to allow the Spirit's freedom in our worship and
prayer. There were no limitations suggesting that certain gifts were
unacceptable or any misconception that some individuals were more

spiritual simply on the basis of giftedness. The absence of any spiritual competition or one-up-manship allowed us the freedom to focus on genuine worship and intercessory prayer.

In that context our numbers have steadily grown over the last few years. An essential ingredient in the signed covenant is a commitment to sponsor various intra-church activities, opportunities which bring the Body of Christ into contact with one another and also allow for public witness. Our first event was a three evening celebration with the author and renewal preacher, the late David Watson. Each gathering contained worship, interpretative dance, drama, and the preaching of the word. At the end of each evening an invitation was given for those who wanted to come to know Christ, those who needed his healing, and those who wanted to be filled with the Spirit.

Since this initial meeting there has been ongoing cooperation in projects such as a prolife rally, training workshops using the resources of all of our churches, a Eucharistic celebration, and various evangelistic missions. To suggest that we have gained the cooperation of all the churches within the city would be untrue. Many pastors feel that our activities are either too charismatic or not charismatic enough. Another group feels that we have given up truth by submerging our doctrinal differences. Still others fear that such activities are the genesis of a new denomination or even the trailings of an apostate ecumenical movement. Some view the activities as subversive to denominational fellowships or the efforts of the Evangelical Fellowship of Canada. However, year by year new pastors are joining in this renewal covenant. The warmth of fellowship, the urgency of intercession, and the nature of worship has bound our hearts together.

This Wednesday gathering has no official name, no hierarchical structure, no planned agenda. Our goal is to place ourselves at the disposal of God, to pray His desires for our city, and to participate with one another with seeing those desires achieved.

The fulfillment of 2 Chronicles 7:14 must begin at the level of pastors and church leaders in every city. As with the ministry of Daniel (Dan. 9:1-19) there must be those representatives who are confessing the sins of God's collective people and seeking his favour for future blessings. The consequences of such intercession and cooperation have been specifically detailed by Jesus. We can expect that the world would believe because we have become one.

Let none of us take Howard Snyder's proposal as outlandish.

Such activities are not out of the realm of possibility. At the same time we should not underestimate the cost and effort of such a venture. The economics and organizational necessities are minimal in comparison with the personal humility that is necessary for the coming together of God's leadership. But is this not what Jesus is asking of us? Seeing Him kneeling before the Father and requesting his petition, can we do less than comply?[2]

RESTORED RELATIONSHIPS

Every other summer I look forward to returning to Texas for a holiday with my parents. Although Texas in the summer months is oppresively hot, going home is an appealing experience. It is appealing because home means unconditional love and loyalty towards me and my family. In this environment it doesn't matter if I have failed or succeeded, I am still loved by people who are loyal to me.

God's family ought to be like this, shouldn't it? Blood ought not to be thicker than the waters of baptism. What is it that produces loyalty and unconditional love in the Christian community? One suggestion is that these qualities emerge when the community disciplines itself in personal relationships. In that context, the fires of revival are free to flow through unhindered channels.

PERSONAL DISCIPLINE

"And if your brother sins, go and reprove him in private; if he listens to you, you have won a brother. But if he does not listen to you, take one or two more with you, so that by the mouth of two or three witnesses every fact may be confirmed" (Matt. 18:15-16). In the context of this passage, Jesus had been speaking to his disciples about leading people to ruin (18:6). He now shifts his attention and talks about rescuing people who are headed for ruin.

For loyalty to emerge in Christian community there must be the self-discipline of going to your brother or sister if you see them in sin. If you see a member of the Christian fellowship obviously missing the mark (the Greek word for sin), so that his conduct is not in keeping with the kingdom of God, then you must go to him. Paul says that the deeds of the flesh are evident (Gal. 5:19), so sin will be so obvious that you need not ask an elder or spiritual mentor to point it out. Anyone who sees the shortcoming is commissioned to go. It is not a responsibility just for the leadership, but any believer who observes the activity. The command to go is in the present tense, meaning that you should go repeatedly to the person if necessary.

There is a textual problem in this verse, for some texts add the words "against you". Peter picks up this thrust in his discussion with Jesus (18:21-35), but the best Greek text omits this phrase, expanding it to sinful attitudes and actions that are not necessarily directed against you, but are obvious to the entire community. It is the self-discipline of correcting one another wherever sin is demonstrated. We are to go and reprove the person. We are to bring to the light the things that they may not have seen, to expose areas which they may want to hide, but which are evident to everyone.

Scripture admonishes us to walk in a spirit of gentleness and humility whenever we are called to confront a brother or sister in sin (Gal. 6:1). We go with questions rather than accusations. We may have read actions wrongly and even misunderstood words. What is needed is a clarification and this can only come through questions. If there are accusations people will be too defensive to give us clarification.

Joshua 22 gives us an excellent example of this need. The Reubenites and the Gadites and the half tribe of Manasseh were appointed portions of the land on the east side of the Jordan. The remaining tribes of Israel were given portions on the west side. The two and a half tribes remaining in the east built an altar for themselves. No sooner had they done this than they were reproached by the remaining representative of Israel. These leaders reprimanded the two and a half tribes for their symbol of apostasy and warned them of the judgement of God. They brought accusations. But as the story unfolds it becomes quite clear that the two and a half tribes meant no statement of idolatry through their building, only an altar which witnessed to the fact that those on the east side of the Jordan worshipped the same God as those on the west side. This was not idolatry, but a statement for later generations to observe that the two and a half tribes did belong to Israel. What was needed in this situation was not accusation but clarification.

With such a simple directive from Jesus, it would be thought that the church would have no difficulty fulfilling these words. But such is not the case. Repeatedly we hear people say, "It is really not my business. I'm hardly qualified morally, not to mention by training, to interfere. Jesus tells us not to judge one another. I need to talk this over with someone. Perhaps it's just a passing thing, something which will go away in time. It's just not done like this in Canada. Besides it would do no good. The person would simply react and be embittered towards me. By the way what constitutes sin anyway?"

I realize that there are often ambiguities that make such an encounter difficult. But it is also true to say that behind our attempts at being humble and tactful is the fact that we are uncommitted cowards. We are "fillet of soul brothers and sisters," Christians with no backbone. We want respectable Christian friendships but we do not want the discomfort of family relationships. We want to be friends, but we do not want to be brothers and sisters. John White says it this way. "Take your pick. Do you choose to be a "Christian" club member or a member of the body of Christ? You cannot have it both ways. If you are a member of Christ's body, you must go to your brother and seek reconciliation. To say that you are not bothered by his sin is to say that you betrayed God's standards and adopted the club's. It is far easier to be a club member than to be a member of the body."[3]

C.S. Lewis once called God the "Transcendental Interferer." We see this so vividly in the incarnation of our Lord Jesus. He saw his brothers and sisters in sin and came to us without condemnation; he brought forgiveness and reconciliation. Not with smug pre-judgement that we would never change, but with a confidence that with his aid we could and would change our behaviour. As followers of Jesus we are to model the theological pattern. We are not to allow people to rest in their sin but to bring them the news of forgiveness and reconciliation.

Do you have one or two Christian friends who have the freedom to speak to you about sin in your own life? Every Christian needs such friends. I have several friends with whom I have much confidence. I have invited them to correct my life at any point in which they feel that I am falling short of the kingdom of God. Because of the mutual invitation for such correction, our relationships are free and accessible to one another. This passage does not demand intimate friendships before we share corrective words, only that we assume the responsibility of going to our brother or sister in humility and gentleness.

MUTUAL DISCIPLINE

Jesus says that our correction of one another is to be done in private, the two alone, "between four eyes." If we have the courage to speak to a person in private it usually means that there is something needed to be corrected. In our privacy a loyalty and security begins to develop. There is a sense that the person really has our welfare in mind. To tell other people before we tell the person who has sinned is to destroy the sincerity of our appeal. It is to tempt the listener to greater offense. Gossip is when we share detrimental information to those who are not part of the problem nor part of the solution. All the listener can do is to be angry and fume with hostility. Our motive is to reconcile and forgive sin and not to see it spread. Therefore we are to go to the person alone.

Occasionally a brother or sister may feel that we are just on their case and that our exposure has little validity. Then, we are to take two or three witnesses along with us. These witnesses will be able to monitor whether or not we are biased in our reproof. They will also be able to give further evidence to the suggestions we had made if needed. The witnesses are not a means of spreading the problem to more people, but as a lever for bringing greater pressure to reconciliation.

PRACTICAL STEPS

In going to another person we want to have a few practical things in mind. We want to make sure that we have bathed the relationship in prayer. We want to make sure that we have examined our own motives and clarified the purpose of the meeting to be the forgiveness and reconciliation. We want to make sure that we have gathered the facts. At this point our criticism of the person needs to be very specific. We need to be cautious of vague generalities and just nit-picking at an insignificant incident. Rather we are looking for facts which communicate an overall picture of the person's attitude or actions.

At this point it might be helpful to write out a few questions which we have in mind. Bill Gothard suggests an opener like this: "I have always wanted to give a good report about you to anyone who asked. For this reason I wish you could explain to me something that I don't understand. Why is it that in your Sunday School class you appear to be so hostile towards John?" We might also come and affirm our love for a brother and sister and then say, "John, it appears to me, that in the last few months you have been extremely negative and critical. Do you think that I have a proper perspective of what is going on in your life?"

It is most important at this time that we allow the person to talk freely. If they ask for helps or suggestions, then we should be prepared to give that also. Our major concern is that we do not appear to have been doing all of the talking. If this is the case then the person will only leave us feeling that they have been preached at rather than questioned. We are only mirrors and not judges. We have come to mediate and reconcile, not condemn.

As spanking serves as a release of the debt of guilt for children, so does confrontation of a Christian who has been sinning. If there is validity in the analysis and the person is prepared to receive the forgiveness that God applies, there is a release of guilt.

Maybe you are asking yourself the question, "Should this person repent of his actions before he is forgiven and what if he should turn around and do the same thing a few minutes later?" It is important to remember that repentance is not ours to exact or to give. Repentance must come from the heart of the person. Our job is to bring forgiveness. Luke records Jesus as saying, "if your brother sins, rebuke him. And if he repents, forgive him. And if he sins against you seven times a day, and returns to you seven times, saying "I repent," then you shall forgive him (Luke 17:3-4).

Occasionally you will be on the receiving end of the criticism. If you have asked for it, be prepared to take it. The posture is not to be defensive but to be quick to hear, slow to speak and slow to anger (James 1:19). Don't let there be pressure to answer all the criticisms. Make sure you get specifics so that you have something to deal with. Ask yourself, "Lord, what are you trying to say to me through this criticism?" Let the whole event become a source of learning. You want to delay your conversation after the first encounter in order to have some reflection on the things that were said. This is legitimate as long as we are not attempting to avoid the criticism. Again, as it is in the case when we go to someone else, their coming to us is to provide restored relationships in a holy community.

CHURCH DISCIPLINE

Occasionally a person who has been spoken to in private and has had the collaboration of several witnesses, is still unrepentant of his attitude and behaviour (Matt. 18:17-20). On this occasion he is to be brought before the entire church. What is the church? Is it the two or three gathered together in Jesus' name? The scope of scriptures suggests that it is not. The church rather is where the word is preached, gifts of the Holy Spirit are exercised, sacraments of baptism and the Lord's supper are practised, where church government operates, and discipline is regulated.

The person is brought to the body of Christ, not just to the elders of the church. The elders are there in order to make sure that the word of God and the Spirit of God are obeyed. However, the responsibility for action lies with the entire body of Christ. In these difficult moments weighing decisions that bear upon the eternal destiny of people, Jesus promises to be close by, imparting strength and direction (Matt. 18:20). We have the confidence that what we forbid on earth is forbidden in heaven, and we also have the confidence that what we permit on earth is also permitted in heaven.

A person expelled from the presence of the community is still a candidate for reconciliation and forgiveness. The very action of the church thrusting the person outside the community is to be a motivating influence to call the person to repentance and to receive God's forgiveness. Although many have read this passage as primarily dealing with throwing people out of the church, the desire of the passage is how to win brothers and sisters back into the Kingdom of God. It is not removing the problem, it is restoring the person.

CANADIAN RECONCILIATION

Charles Colson tells an interesting story of his speaking at the National Prayer breakfast in Ottawa several years ago. After he spoke on the need to be reconciled to our enemies, John Diefenbaker and Pierre Trudeau went straight towards each other, hugged one another and asked for forgiveness.[4] Surely if these political enemies could be restored to one another, members of the body of Christ in Canada can do the same.

Proverbs 16:28 says that a "perverse man spreads strife, and a slanderer separates intimate friends. But a man or woman who restores a brother or sister from sin is a bridge builder for loyalty and unconditional love" (*Living Letters*). Such an environment in Canada would not only be inviting to Christians but also to onlooking non-Christians. Let the church be restored in unity in order that the glory of Christ might be spread among our nation.

1 Howard A. Snyder, *Community of the King*, (Downers Grove: Inter-Varsity Press, 1977), pp.179-180.
2 George Mallone, "Public Rallies Foster Unity," (*Eternity*, January, 1982) pp. 52-53.
3 John White, *Eros Defiled*, (Downers Grove: Inter-Varsity Press, 1977) p.159.
4 David Mainse, *God Keep Our Land*, (Toronto: Mainroads Productions, 1981) pp.73-74.

Chapter 10

PRAY TILL THE POWER COMES DOWN

"When God intends great things for his people, he sets them to pray." This word, or something very similar to it, has been repeated over and over by people who know how God works during revival. Prayer paves the way for revival, smooths out the rough places in revival and preserves the fruit of revival. Prayer is indispensable in revival.

So far, there would be little disagreement. The point of conflict is whether or not we are prepared to spend time in this intercessory ministry. Over the last few years, pastors in the Wednesday morning prayer fellowship have spent hundreds of hours praying for revival in Canada. However, we know the shallowness of our commitment in this area. Constantly there are conflicts of schedule and busy work which preclude our involvement. The excuses I have received from pastors who on one hand "long for revival," but have no time for prayer, would make an excellent cartoon book for a coffee table.

If two things stand out in my mind as a result of our trip across Canada, the first would be the division of believers, and the second would be the lack of prayer across the country. Thankfully there are some who are praying for the country. I think of the women in small Bible studies throughout Canada who meet weekly and pray, as well as some organizational prayer chains which are involved in this ministry. But one must lament the lack of pastors and church leaders gathering to pray for the nation. The few groups that we did see at prayer seemed quite caught up in the pride of their own personal spirituality and seemed to have missed the brokenness that characterizes the true work of God.

But I'm afraid that the problem is bigger than this. I believe that today many pastors have become agnostics. They still believe in Jesus and affirm that he has come into their life, but the vitality seems to be gone and the assurance of answered prayer is also lacking. A young pastor said to me, "I can't get into praying for revival. It doesn't work. I have prayed and nothing has happened." I can empathize with such feelings, but I also know that God wants us to meet him in prayer and to pray his concerns for the nation. It is God's prerogative as to the timing and answer of these prayers, but I am to pray. We can also say from scripture and church history that wherever God's people begin to pray faithfully and in repentance, revival is not far away.

MODEL ONE: A REFORMATION LEADER

Bob Birch is a man who has committed his life to prayer and especially to the reviving of the church in Canada. Here are his own words and concerns for this subject:

"One early morning I was going through the private and searching process of repenting before God. I longed to be effective and fruitful for Christ's sake, and had written down a list of my shortcomings which I felt were quenching the Spirit and hurting God's children. The Lord who moved me to confession accepted my repentance, and confirmed this by directing me to consider two models for prayer and the revival of Canada.

"First, is the model of *King Hezekiah* (2 Kings 18). Hezekiah was convinced that his success and the success of Israel's kingdom depended on intimate communion with God which centered in the temple. Cleansing must begin at once from the idolatry and demonic powers that had gained access under his father's rule. Boldly he broke in pieces the bronze snake Moses had made and to which Israel now burnt incense. Hezekiah ordered the Levites: 'Consecrate yourselves now and consecrate the temple of the Lord, the God of your fathers. Remove all defilement from the sanctuary. Our fathers were unfaithful; they did evil in the eyes of the Lord our God and forsook him' (2 Chron. 29:5, 6).

"The young king surely had visions of restoring the glory of God to the temple, as it had been when the priests under Solomon brought the Ark of God to the inner sanctuary. 'Then the temple of the Lord was filled with a cloud, and the priests could not perform their service because of the cloud, for the glory of the Lord filled the temple of God' (2 Chron. 5:13, 14). We call these Old Testament events 'types and shadows,' but they were more than that. They put us to shame. They were the manifestations of a divine presence and power which we in these last days should know experientially in surpassing measure.

"Our most earnest prayer should be for the holy awareness and manifestation of the presence of God the Spirit in our midst. Isaiah's vision of the Lord filling the temple, and John's vision of the radiant Christ in the midst of the churches became for them the norm by which they measured the spiritual temperature of the people of God. Revival is a sovereign visitation of the Lord in his temple, but he expects us through prayer and obedience, to prepare our hearts for his coming in power.

"Next, we find that Hezekiah *restored prayer, praise and worship to the temple.* 'Hezekiah gave the order to sacrifice the burnt offering on the altar. As the offering began, singing to the Lord began also, accompanied by trumpets and the instruments of David. The whole assembly bowed in worship, while the singers and the trumpeters played. All this continued until the sacrifice of the burnt offering was completed....the king and everyone present with him knelt down and worshipped' (2 Chron. 5:12).

"We pray dutifully, 'Thy will be done on earth as it is done in heaven,' but we are fearfully inhibited from actually doing the worship scripture enjoins (Rev. 5:8). My years of experience as a pastor tell me that the carnal mind of Christians resolutely resists worship. Freedom in prayer and worship are the thermometer of our spiritual temperature. Effective prayer and praise cannot be separated. I will never forget being literally shaken to the roots of my being as I stood with 3300 delegates from 70 nations along with thousands of Koreans, in the Young Nak Presbyterian Church in Seoul, Korea as we lifted our hearts and voices in uninhibited praise and prayer to God. The heights of heaven and the ends of the earth came together in an unforgettable, overwhelming of divine love and intercession.

"The history of the Church bears witness to revival always finding expression in fresh creative praise and prayer. Paul and Silas knew it when bound and bleeding in prison, 'while praying, they were also singing praises to God,' thus releasing power from heaven to break open the prison with an earthquake and save the jailor and his family (Acts 16:25). Praise God, that where the Spirit of renewal is again flowing in power, love songs to Jesus our Lord are releasing love to one another and a powerful witness to the world. May it increase across Canada, breaking through our carnal reserves that are earthly, unspiritual and fearful. Only people penetrated and intoxicated by the Spirit are really free to be adequate witnesses to Jesus Christ (Eph. 5:18-20).

"Next, Hezekiah led a bold, *united, spiritual movement.* The king with the hearty support of his leaders called for a great Passover festival in Jerusalem. Invitations were sent even to the northern separated tribes. They read in part, 'Do not be stiff-necked, as your fathers were; submit to the Lord. Come to the sanctuary, which he has consecrated forever. Serve the Lord your God, so that his fierce anger will turn away from you' (2 Chron. 30:18). Many scoffed but, 'in Judah the hand of God was on the people to give them unity to mind.'

"The Spirit of God's grace and truth moved through the land like a strong wind. It was a heart-moving time, for although many through negligence were not ceremonially prepared: 'yet they ate the Passover, contrary to what was written. But Hezekiah prayed for them saying, "May the Lord who is good, pardon everyone who sets his heart on seeking God — the Lord, the God of his fathers — even if he is not clean according to the rules of the sanctuary." And the Lord heard Hezekiah and healed the people' (2 Chron. 30:18-20). They kept the Passover in the wrong month, and they observed it for two weeks instead of one. But there was 'great joy in Jerusalem' and 'God heard them for their prayer reached heaven, His holy dwelling place.'

"Our own worldly characters and self-interests are too strong to ever make unity possible, but God has given us his own glory, his presence, his Spirit (John 17). We should then examine all our doctrinal statements, all our constitutional procedures, and all our historical traditions in the light of Christ's prayer and presence. The grace of God in Hezekiah brought mercy and compassion, unity and healing. Christ is not divided, he alone achieved our redemption and he alone is Head of the Church. Let us humble ourselves and come together on our knees. To be one as the Father and Son are one, however 'impossible' to achieve, must be the opening and closing thought of all our plans related to the Church of Jesus Christ.

"In this regard we should thank God for the recent International Prayer Assembly call in Seoul, Korea. Co-chairman Vonette Bright made this opening statement:

> For generations, the Church has focused on evangelism by sponsoring events, planning strategy, and rightly investing enormous amounts of money. To our knowledge, none of these efforts have developed a worldwide prayer strategy for evangelism and spiritual awakening. The International Prayer Assembly is, so far as we know, the first international gathering focusing on prayer for spiritual awakening and fulfillment of the Great Commission. Matthew 28:18-20.
>
> We trust that this International Prayer Assembly will build confidence in the power of prayer to affect world situations. The Assembly will hopefully enable international Christian prayer leaders to spur worldwide prayer movements for spiritual awakening, leading to world evangelization. It will emphasize and demonstrate urgency, effectiveness and mobilization procedures for international prayer.

"Next, Hezekiah led in a *national reformation.* Following this powerful movement of repentance and worship, 'the Israelites who were there went out to the towns of Judah, smashed the sacred stones, and cut down the Asherah (poles to a female goddess). They destroyed the high places and the altars throughout the land' (2 Chron 31:1).

"United prayer, in the freedom and power of the Spirit, filled with the word of God, is a mighty lever in the hand of God and man to move heaven and earth. As Paul Bilheimer has said, 'God has placed the enforcement of Calvary's victory in the hands of the church ... but this delegated authority is wholly inoperative apart from the praying of a believing church. Therefore, prayer is where the action is."

"To pray in an all-night prayer meeting with ten thousand Korean Christians, 'lifting up their voices to God with one accord' is a shaking experience. It is the answer of the Korean church to the ever-present threat of the invasion of Communism from the North.

"Satan's strategy in Canada, to withstand the power of prayer, is to seduce and infiltrate the church with worldliness and unbelief. Thank God that there are signs of awakening. In thousands of home fellowships across the land, Christians are calling out to God. National prayer chains such as 'The Great Commission Prayer League', 100 Huntley Street, plus many others are making Christians more prayer conscious.

"While attending the annual conference of the Evangelical Fellowship of Canada in Ottawa I was alerted to the significant effect upon government that an informed praying minority can have, especially when this prayer power is linked with a wise strategy of addressing national moral issues by timely letter writing and with knowledgeable men and women representing God's word in national moral issues.

"While seeking God's face after the conference was over, the Spirit pointed me to the powerful prayer model of Esther and Mordecai before King Xerxes in the Kingdom of Babylon. Here a persecuted, powerless minority triumphed gloriously through fasting and prayer led by Esther. Mordecai was held in high esteem, 'because he worked for the good of his people and spoke up for the welfare of all the Jews.'

"My conclusion is that we need pioneers in the strategy of prayer who are full of faith, and pacesetters of God's promises. The church needs to be patiently and skillfully taught to pray. Changing structural forms and methods, sharpening management skills and redesigning strategies won't cut it without God's power.

"Last, we must reflect upon Hezekiah in the *crucible of conflict*. Two major confrontations with evil faced Hezekiah after his triumphant start. The first of these was the invasion by the defiant heathen King Sennacherib of Assyria. He came to the very walls of Jerusalem. The second was Satan's attack on the king's body so that he gets the message, 'set your house in order because you will die, you will not recover' (2 Chron. 15:38).

"The relationship of all this to prayer is that once we seriously engage the kingdom of darkness, Satan will fight back, for we are challenging his control of our culture with its demonic darkness of a thousand types (Eph. 6:12). God will allow these evil powers to test us to the limit, so that we might grow strong in spirit and overcome them. We will be tempted and tried in every conceivable and unexpected way: health, family, friends, reputation and church associations. Why, because we have determined to know nothing but Christ and him crucified, and we must take up our cross and follow him through our own Gethsemane and Calvary.

"After all this success Hezekiah became self-confident and proud and acted unwisely in regard to envoys sent by the rulers of Babylon. For the scripture says, 'God left him to test him and to know everything that was in his heart' (2 Chron. 32:31). Each of us must ask with fear and trembling, 'Lord, show me what is in my heart.' Do you know your own heart and its potential for evil apart from the very Presence of God?"

MODEL TWO: A GREAT INTERCESSOR

"The cry of my heart now, and has been for many years is, 'Lord, teach us to pray as Daniel prayed (Daniel 9:1-23).' As I long to know what made him an effective intercessor, I notice four qualities, and hence my second model for prayer.

"First, I notice his deep, *Spirit-guided study and meditation of the scriptures* (9:12). We greatly need to 'rightly divide' the Bible with pure hearts and clear heads as we ponder what is happening around us today. As we read the Word and persevere in prayer we are enabled to press so close to God by the Spirit that our own self-consciousness and the presence of Christ meet face to face. We then are thinking and feeling as he does at that moment. At this point we gain great boldness to address him with the issue at hand (9:19).

"Second, effective intercession is *disciplined work*. 'So I gave my attention to the Lord God to seek him by prayer and supplications, with fasting, sackcloth and ashes (9:3).' As Paul says of Epaphras, we need people who are 'always wrestling in prayer' (Col. 4:12).

"God is looking for those who will allow their hearts to be the prayer room of the Holy Spirit (Rom. 8:27-28). Too often we close the door on him and go about our own business, before he has had time to complete his work in and through us. 'Spiritual work is taxing and men are loath to do it. True praying costs an outlay of serious attention and time, which flesh and blood do not relish.'[1]

"Today, the Canadian church is selfishly fat and lazy, unable to pray with passion. Thus, the rivers of living water are reduced to a trickle. Let us repent, change our mind, and press through the open door of revival set before us (Rev. 3:8).

"Third, Daniel's intercession was effective because he *never took Satan's side as the 'accuser of the brethren.'* Never once in his long prayer does he point the finger and say 'they.' Always it is 'we have sinned' or 'my sin and the sin of my people.'

"It is cheap and easy to throw stones at the church and I never want to participate in such activities. Each of us, however, in one way or another, bear some responsibility for its condition. We would do far better to weep than to condemn. Jesus wept over Jerusalem, but at the same time his love flamed with anger against its religious teachers who had driven the spirit of prayer from the temple.

"If the Spirit of effective intercession is to return to the Lord's temple, we must learn to humble our critical, unbelieving mind under God's covenant word to us, even as Daniel did. Take a steady look at our religious talk, and lack of obedience, and beseech God for mercy. He waits to be merciful.

A letter, discovered in an old trunk in the basement of one of my wife's relatives, described a heaven-sent revival in the district of Nellore, India in July, 1906. The letter was recorded by a Miss Dormstadt of the American Baptist Missionary Society and showed the two edges of confession and intercession in revival.

> The revival began last night among our dear girls, and there was awful agony of soul and crying unto God for mercy. Today was given up to prayer — all work suspended. It has been a day of prayer and fasting. The morning was awful — such agony as some of the girls were in, and such a struggle as they passed through before peace came. But oh, the afternoon, with the joy and thanksgiving, confessions and testimony! It was both meat and drink and we tarried in the church from 9:00 a.m. to 6:00 p.m. without coming out. We tried to close from 5:00 to 6:00p.m. but we were not leading. The Blessed Spirit had His own time for closing, and we praise Him for keeping control. It has been a great day, a Great Feast Day. The meetings go on tomorrow. How much longer I do not know. We are just being led.
>
> Such a spirit of confession! The meetings increase in power. It is all so glorious, so wonderful. If all the joys of all my Christmas days were lumped together, it could not begin to equal the joy I am experiencing now. Praise God for His goodness!

"Fourth, deeply strengthened by the Spirit and the word of God, *Daniel persevered for 21 days against a heavy cloud of oppression.* 'At that time I, Daniel, mourned for three weeks. I ate no choice food; no meat or wine touched my lips; and I used no lotions at all until the three weeks were over' (10:2,3).

"Finally, it was in great weakness that *Daniel's prayers broke through* in the spiritual warfare, and God was able to release a heavenly messenger with the words, 'Do not be afraid, O man highly esteemed, Peace! Be strong now; be strong' (10:19).

"The apostle Paul accurately describes the nature of our enemy in this heavenly warfare. 'For we are not fighting against people made of flesh and blood, but against persons without bodies — the evil rulers of the unseen world, those mighty satanic beings and great evil princes of darkness who rule this world; and against huge numbers of wicked spirits in the spirit world' (Eph. 6:12).

"Paul also knew how effective Christian intercessors must arm their minds for the conflict. 'Not in accordance with mere human considerations are we waging warfare against evil, for the weapons of our warfare are not human, but mighty in God's sight, resulting in the demolition of fortresses, demolishing reasonings and every haughty, mental elevation which lifts itself up against the experiential knowledge of God, and leading captive every thought into the obedience to Christ' (2 Cor. 10:4, 5, Wuest).

"We are generally unaware how vulnerable we are to Satan's attacks. Peter learned this the hard way. Confidently he affirmed, 'Though all should forsake you, I will not.' He could not believe Christ's words, that before the cock crowed twice, he would deny Jesus three times. That very night in the garden Peter fell asleep while Jesus kept awake in the battle of prayer. When they walked out of the garden a few hours later, Jesus, controlled by the Spirit offered Himself without spot to God, while Peter denied him with curses.

"To all of us in this heavenly conflict the Lord says, 'Watch and pray that you enter not into temptation; the Spirit is willing, but the flesh is weak' (Matt. 26:41). Thank God your spirit is willing! Keep willing for God and he will work in you his good pleasure' (Phil. 2:13)."

NOW, TO WORK

You have now read these clear exhortations by Bob Birch. What steps will you take? Is there time to set aside for personal intercession? When will you do it? Are you to meet with others to pray for revival? When will you do it and with whom? Do you need to learn more about this ministry? Where and to whom can you go to learn about intercession? Whatever you do, don't just read this book and set it back on your shelf. To do so will grieve the Holy Spirit and hinder the work of God in this nation.

1   As quoted in Dick Eastman, *No Easy Road*, (Grand Rapids: Baker House, 1971), p. 12.

Chapter 11

DON'T BOW THE KNEE!

When I came to, I was in a dark alley. As I looked down I noticed that I was wearing heavy brown workboots which I could not remember buying. Neither could I remember buying the double wool workpants I was wearing. Next my hands felt my coat and for the first time it was something familiar, my dark wool topcoat. Next, my hands slid to my furlined hat and I said to myself, "This is just like the one Bob bought in Calgary."

I decided to step out of the alley into the light. As I did, I could see that it had begun to snow. I had a chill run down the middle of my back and I said to myself, "It feels like winter all over the earth."

Shortly I heard a dog bark and retreated into the shadows for protection. In a few minutes two policemen with their dog walked by. They wore fur hats with tall dark boots and heavy grey coats. You could tell the coldness of the night from their nostrils.

I walked into the street and tried to determine exactly where I was. I walked down a few blocks and saw a light coming from a building. As I entered I was immediately aware that it was a British pub. No one seemed to pay any attention to my entrance, so I sat down by myself. The bar mistress came over and asked me what I would have to drink; "A pint of bitter," I replied. Shortly she returned with my drink and sat down next to me. "You're a stranger aren't you?" "I am", I replied. "Do you need a place to stay for the night?" was her next question. "I do," I said.

After I finished my drink, she showed me upstairs to the room.

Standing at the entrance I decided to make some inquiry where I was. "Is there a priest in the city?" I said. "A priest! What do you want a priest for?" Although it was not true, I felt I needed to tell her, "I think I'm dying." She said there was one priest remaining and that she would show me where he was the following morning.

That night I curled up in my bed with my boots, pants and hat still on, fearing the policemen and their dog would return.

The following morning, the lady showed me out to an old stone church. As I walked up the stone covered steps, I noticed that it had begun to snow again and once more a chill came up the middle of my back and I said, "It feels like winter all over the earth."

The secretary escorted me into the priest's office and I looked about for evidence of where I was and when it was. There was no clue to my searching.

In a few minutes an Anglican priest walked into the office. I began to make small talk to break the ice. "I once knew some Anglican priests. Did you know David Watson, Michael Green, Michael Harper or John Stott?"

"They're all dead," he said matter of factly.

"Most of those men were awfully young to have died," I said.

"They did not die of natural causes my young man. They all died in the purge of '84 when they would not bow the knee." I had no idea what he was talking about so I remained silent. "What can I do for you?" the priest asked.

"Well, I have a problem. You see, I don't know who I am, I don't know where I am and I don't know how I got here."

"You're not British!" he said accusingly.

"No, I'm a Canadian" I replied.

"Good god, man! What are you doing here?" he shouted.

"I don't know" I said. "I've just come here to ask for your help."

"I know who you are, you're one of those Canadian detainees."

"Detainee?"

"Sure. In the purge of '84 those in Britain who would not bow the knee were executed. The Canadians who would not bow the knee were deported here to work in the mines. The reason you can't remember anything is because they cut out part of your brain. You've got to get out of here this very minute, unless the police find you. There's only one church left and we don't want it closed down."

He showed me to the office door and as I walked out the door I noticed that it had begun to snow again. As the repeated chill ran down my back I once again said to myself, "It feels like winter has just come to the whole earth."

JUST A DREAM?

Where did this vision come from? I must admit that when it came to me in these exact words I had been in bed with a running fever of one hundred and three degrees for three days. Maybe I was delirious. I realize now that several factors led to its development. First, I had no food for three days straight and my spiritual sensitivities had been heightened by this involuntary fast. Second, in the back of my subconscious was the foreboding of an Orwellian "1984". We had just entered that eventful year when I had this vision and I had just completed the rereading of Orwell's famous book by the same title. Third, was the growing conviction that Canadians had too easily been seduced by their governments to bow the knee to unrighteous laws. Winter comes to earth when governments make immoral demands of its citizens, but springtime endures when righteousness reigns among governments and its peoples.

SHADRACH, MESHACH AND ABED-NEGO

Daniel 3 records for us the heroic tale of three young men who refused to bow the knee during the purge of the Babylonian king Nebuchadnezzar. They had been ordered to fall down and worship a ninety foot statue, probably of Nebuchadnezzar, in the plain of Dura. When they refused this order they were brought before the king to give an explanation.

Nebuchadnezzar was angry. You could see it in his face (3:13,19). These three, upon whom he had lavished special attention (1:1-16), had now betrayed his kindness. Unwilling to condemn them on heresay evidence, the king brings them in for a second chance.

"Boys, I have this new rule. I expect you to obey it just like everyone else in my realm. When you hear the music (3:5) I expect you to bow down and worship the image I have set up. If you don't, then you can test out my new furnace which I have just built for this occasion."

What was Nebuchadnezzar asking for by this gesture? Was it religious homage or political uniformity? Notice that it was demanded of all the conquered people (v.4). There certainly was no religious ecumenism among these people, so any attempt to impose mass religious conversion would be insane.

No, this gesture was one of swearing absolute loyalty to Nebuchadnezzar. It was a commitment to obey his word at all times. No doubt this action had religious overtones, but essentially it was a test of loyalty.

The problem with the test was that it contravened God's revealed law. God's word through Moses was very clear that Israel was not to have any gods before Yahweh. They were to make no graven images of any gods nor were they to worship and serve these gods (Ex. 20:3-5).

TO OBEY OR DISOBEY, THAT IS THE QUESTION

When is it wrong to obey governments? It is wrong when governments demand obedience to laws which contravene God's will as revealed in Holy Scripture. Governments do not have the right to demand immoral actions from its citizens. To do such is to forfeit its right to govern and to legitimize disobedience.

Most Canadian Christians have been raised with a passivity towards governments. They have not wanted to be part of the lawless age (2 Tim.3:1-4). They have misunderstood Romans 13 to say that God ordains particular governments, rather than the institution of government, and these governments even when evil is not to be resisted. This, coupled with a general displeasure of the whole notion of civil disobedience, has smothered Christians from protesting immoral legislation.

But there is, as this passage suggests, biblical precedent for civil disobedience. This is a working assumption among Christians in totalitarian regimes and we should expect that it might be necessary in democracies where humanism rules.

Shadrach, Meshach and Abed-nego had no other choice than to disobey the word of the king (3:28). Fortunately, in Canada we have a number of options in protesting immoral laws before we are forced to civil disobedience.

First, we can protest through *elected representatives*. The preamble to our new constitution states, "Whereas Canada is founded upon principles that recognize the supremacy of God and the rule of law." We must elect men and women to office who believe that statement. Christians must not elect people solely on the basis of economic theory. It is righteousness that exalts a nation (Prov.

14:34) and not economic theory. These representatives should be held accountable for their votes and made aware when legislation contravenes the moral requirements demanded of a Christian.

Second, Christians can *lobby* and make their opinion known on moral issues. The saying that the "majority are not silent, the government is deaf" is a funny line but not true. Democratic governments are sensitive to public opinion, but Christians refuse to get involved. Time and time again we hear from politicians who say that if they had ten letters from their constituents they would vote differently on a piece of legislation.

Third, we can *litigate*. We can go before the courts and argue against a piece of legislation. Are you prepared to contribute to legal funds in order to take a stand for righteousness? People who have no belief in God and who maintain a relativistic ethic know that this is what has to be done for their own cause and they are pouring millions of dollars into legal funds to see their opinions enshrined as law.

Fourth, we can *flee the country*. If the laws are impossible to obey then we can take the route patterned by many of our forefathers, we can escape to a land where there is freedom and respect for moral law.

Fifth, non-violently, we can *disobey the government and then submit to the punishment* they have decreed for violators. Governments have the right to punish law breakers and we acknowledge that right. Christians always submit, either to the law itself or to the punishment for violating that law.

IT MAY BE LEGAL, BUT IT'S NOT RIGHT

The history of the Christian church is full of men and women who were consumed with God's righteousness and bravely announced to the authorities that "It may be legal, but it's not right." They stood up to unjust laws and combated them with various tactics.

John Wesley countered the argument that slavery was a legitimate business practice by saying: "Can human law turn darkness into light or evil into good? Notwithstanding ten thousand laws, right is right and wrong is wrong still. . . . . I absolutely deny all slave-holding to be consistent with any degree of even natural justice."[1]

Lord Shaftesbury, who tirelessly worked for the rights of children and women in the "white slavery" markets of Britain, revealed his reason for protesting this injustice in the House of Commons: "I have been bold enough to undertake this task, because I must regard the objects of it as being created, like ourselves, by the same Master, redeemed by the same Saviour, and destined to the same immortality."[2]

Such concern can also be seen in the Christian passion of John Howard and Elizabeth Fry in their concern for people incarcerated in prisons. Canon Overton, although not sympathetic to the evangelical cause, knew what motivated the conscience of these evangelicals: "to be serious and to be Evangelical were only different ways of saying the same thing. It would be no exaggeration to say that, morally and spiritually, the dominant religious power, both inside and outside the Church of England, at the close of the eighteenth century, was that which was evoked by the Evangelical Revival."[3]

The French statesman, Alexis de Tocqueville, upon his return from America wrote these words on American policy and culture: "I sought for the greatness and genius of America in her commodious harbours and her ample rivers, and it was not there... I sought for the greatness and genius of America in her democratic Congress and her matchless constitution, and it was not there. Not until I went into the churches of America and heard her pulpits flame with righteousness did I understand the secret of her genius and power."[4]

In each analysis there was the overwhelming conviction that God had spoken in righteousness and although the law of the land said otherwise, it was not right and needed to be protested. It was legal but it was not right.

CANADIAN CONCERNS

Are there issues in Canada today that should stir us to action? Most definitely. Why? Because our judicial and legislative systems are now governing out of sociological law rather than law which acknowledges the supremacy of God and revealed morality. Law today is based upon popular appeal which is subject to the whims of the constituency. As with Oliver Wendell Holmes, Canadian governments now practice the principle that "truth is the majority vote of that nation that could lick all others."[5]

What are the issues that should stir us to action?

First, is the issue of unrestricted *abortion* practised in the hospitals of this country. If Dr. Henry Morgentaler wins his case before the courts, Canada will have coast to coast abortion clinics and no doubt you and I will be asked to finance these abortions through our contributions to the medical services plan. Before God can we possibly contribute to the wholesale destruction of human life?

Second, the tentative view of the mentally *handicapped* should also be one of our major concerns. Several years ago, in the province of British Columbia, the case of Stephen Dawson made the headlines of our daily newspapers. In a lower court ruling the parents of Stephen Dawson were allowed to prevent the implantation of shunts to relieve pressure on his brain. Many of my friends working with the mentally handicapped confessed at the time, "If they let Stephen die they might as well kill all handicapped children, for there are many worse off than he." Later a higher court reversed that decision. As one read of the responses of the two judges it was as though they were dealing from different decks of cards. One was arguing from sociological law while the other was arguing from a Judaeo-Christian ethic. On that occasion moral law was victor, but we might not win again. What will you do if we begin to lose cases like Stephen Dawson? Will we sit back passively and say, "It's the law, it must be okay"?

Third is a concern for *persecuted believers* throughout the world. Our government continues to have warm economic relationships with governments which persecute and imprison thousands of believing Christians. It seems more of a priority to sell our products than to protest this inhumanity.

Fourth, *nuclear warfare* is another important issue and one in which Canadian Christians are divided. Personally, if it were possible to do so, I would participate in conventional warfare to defend the freedoms of this land. I am not a pacifist, although I have sympathy with that position. As to the question of whether or not nuclear weapons actually deter the aggressors, sometimes I think yes and other times no. But as to the use of nuclear arms to kill innocent non-combatants, I am a nuclear pacifist. As the respected evangelical Anglican John Stott has said: "every Christian, whatever he may think of the possibility of a 'just' use of conventional weapons, must be a nuclear pacifist."[6] Canada has maintained a reputation as a world peace-maker throughout the years. Surely this is a time when Christians will want to encourage that role in international affairs to continue.

There are many other areas that deserve our concern. You would not be happy to visit the inside of our prisons and observe the things that are going on in our criminal system. Neither can we sit back in ease with the present attitude towards pornography laws which are clearly on the books but not being enforced by any level of government. There are proposals in certain political parties in this country that prostitution be legalized and be given districts within our cities to be operated. Racism is a smoldering fire which could erupt in our cities at any time but is not being addressed. Educational policies are tending to the persuasion that children belong to the society and not to the parents and can be educated any way the society chooses. Economic hardship is creating a new poverty class, a problem that many provincial governments are ignoring. These issues need a clear Christian response.

A GREAT DELIVERANCE

The story of Shadrach, Meshach and Abed-nego ends on a triumphant note. Although the three were tossed into Nebuchadnezzar's furnace, they were marvelously preserved by God (3:24-30). Such a deliverance caused the king to side with the three men and to provide for their prosperity. The powerful demonstration of Israel's God altered the response of Nebuchadnezzar's powerful government.

The principles of this passage are very clear. When Canadians yield up their bodies of righteousness (3:28), God goes into the furnace with us and from there is able to bring a great deliverance. And when we take such a stand for righteousness, God even makes our enemies to be at peace with us (Prov. 16:7).

As I write these words we are on the eve of a federal election. Each of the leading candidates seems to stroke for popular appeal while discharging moral responsibility in the crucial areas. Even after the election, most likely parliament will have only a few active Christians, men and women who stand for righteousness no matter what the personal cost. The forces of unrighteousness are posing a respectable face and want the weight of law to suppress any light left in this nation.

Now is the moment for Canadian revival. Now is the time to pray for awakening. Now is the time for God to reveal his mighty hand. Now is the time for believers to enter the furnace.

1 J.W. Beady, *This Freedom Whence?*, (New York: American Tract Society, 1944) p.142.
2 Ibid., p.219.
3 Ibid., p.205.
4 Leon Jaworski, *Crossroads*, (Elgin, Illinois: David C. Cook, 1981) p.128.
5 Francis A. Schaeffer and C. Everett Koop, *Whatever Happened To The Human Race*, (Old Tappan, New Jersey: Fleming H. Revell Company, 1978) p.25.
6 Ronald J. Sider and Richard K. Taylor, *Nuclear Holocaust And Christian Hope*, (Downers Grove, Ill.: Intervarsity Press, 1982) p.66.

Chapter 12

CONSIDER YOUR WAYS!

About twenty years ago, the elderly German billionaire Daniel K. Ludwig decided to grow trees in the Amazon jungle, much like a farmer would raise wheat in Saskatchewan. But after a one billion dollar investment, the plantation at Jari is now up for sale. At the peak work load it employed seventy-four hundred people, used six thousand water buffalo and planted one hundred and twenty million trees. But now Jari has been labelled a "counterfeit paradise." Under the thick lush canopy there was a nutrient poor soil and apparently Ludwig and his assistants failed to take adequate soil samples at the beginning, thus the growth rate was seventy-five percent less than expected.

CANADIAN SOIL: RICH OR POOR?

God alone knows the condition of the Canadian soil for revival. If it is unreceptive soil, no amount of human energy or money can make it productive. If, however, the soil is receptive to revival, then God expects us to carry out the mandate of this generation to make his name known.

There are signs that the soil is ready for planting and that a great harvest will be reaped. Economic discomfort is causing many to reinvestigate the priorities of life. Family stress is encouraging people to ask if there is something which can hold family units together. The threat of nuclear holocaust leaves every Canadian nervous about the decade of the eighties. The church in America is flexing its muscles and showing signs of longing for reformation. Such an upswing would no doubt spill into Canada. For the materialist who is concerned with personal peace and prosperity the outlook is gloomy, but to the Christian who sees the hand of God bringing this nation to its knees, the prospect of renewal is glorious.

But the question we must ask is whether or not we care enough to pay the price for Canadian revival. The soil appears ready. God appears willing to respond to a repentant nation. Are we ready to cooperate with his plan for the nation?

A COVENANT FOR REVIVAL

As you come to the last pages of this book, how will you respond to the call for Canadian revival?

May I suggest that you take your Bible, a notebook and spend at least an hour in prayer and reflection upon the following ten statements. Let this serve as your personal summary of all the previous chapters.

First, a prayer of commitment:

> "Lord you placed me in Canada for a purpose. I affirm that you love this country and its people.
>
> I confess that I have failed you in many ways and stand in need of your forgiveness.
>
> I desire to turn from my wicked ways and to seek your priorities for my life and this nation.
>
> Be gracious to us and extend your loving hand.
>
> Revive your church, that we might rejoice in you and bear witness to other Canadians.
>
> We ask this solely that you might be glorified in this nation as well as in all the nations of the world.
>
> Lord, in order to see Canada revived, I need to do my part. What would you have me to do in these areas?"

1. I see the need of spending more time with you in personal communion, therefore I . . . .

2. I see the need of praying more for my home, church, city and nation, therefore I . . . .

3. I believe that you want purified and reconciled relationships within your body, therefore I . . . .

4. I believe that you want the body of Christ to be one in every city, therefore I.......

5. I know that you will not bless sinful rebellion on my part, therefore I repent of.......

6. I believe that the renewal of your church will come only with a mighty filling of the Holy Spirit, therefore I.......

7. I know that man centered tradition in the church can be a major hindrance to the work of your kingdom, therefore I.......

8. I know that Satan does not want your church to come alive and would do all in his power to bring it to its knees, therefore I.......

9. I believe there is a cost to be paid for the renewal of the church, therefore I.......

10. Not only does Canada need to see your glory but the entire world also, therefore I.......

May God richly bless your sincere concerns for his Kingdom in Canada and may he revive his church or come and rescue it from all its evil.